Intuitive Interpreting

A Spanish Medical Dictionary Mastered for the Professional Interpreter

Annalisa Nash Fernandez

Ethnic Ethos Books
Domain Americas LLC
PO Box 141453
Coral Gables, FL 33134 USA

ISBN: 0692362932
ISBN-13: 978-0692362938 (Ethnic Ethos Books)

INTUITIVE INTERPRETING

CONTENTS

FOREWORD

Entre las distintas ciencias que están desarrolladas hoy en día una de las más importantes para la vida cotidiana es la medicina, cuya finalidad esencial es la salud de las personas del mundo, que se manifiestan de distintas formas, como también en distintos idiomas. Por lo que para lograr una mejor medicina debemos trabajar en conseguir todo aquello que mejore el eje central de la misma, el cual es la relación médico-paciente.

La medicina es una constante traducción entre las palabras del dolor del paciente y la comprensión de la dolencia. Es de tarea de todos los médicos hacer esta traducción interna en las que las palabras del paciente se vuelven herramientas en este proceso de acompañamiento mutuo.

Ser parte de este proyecto, es ser parte de la búsqueda del método más eficaz para la traducción del inglés-español en el ámbito de la medicina. En situaciones puntuales de la realidad diaria médica, un diccionario eficaz y práctico, realizado por y para intérpretes, es una herramienta invaluable y necesaria.

La terminología médica en español está basado en el griego y en el latín, con una abundancia de cognados con el inglés. Son fácilmente reconocibles para los que conocen el léxico de la medicina. Este diccionario procura ser la respuesta inmediata a nuestros problemas de interpretación de las demás palabras en la manera más efectiva posible, gracias a inclusión de terminología de distintas partes del mundo hispano-parlante, permitiendo que el uso de las palabras que ya reconocemos simplifique nuestra actividad profesional.

Francisco Oddone, M.D.
Universidad Católica de Córdoba, Argentina

Among the many disciplines of modern science, medicine is one of the more important in daily life, as its essential objective is the good health of people worldwide. It manifests itself in many ways, and also in various languages. As a result, to best achieve this objective, we need to focus on that which improves the fundamentals of medicine, which is the doctor-patient relationship.

Medicine is an ongoing translation between the patient's words of pain and the understanding of that pain. It is the responsibility of all doctors to make this internal translation one in which the patient's words become tools in the process of this mutual journey.

Taking part in this project is taking part in the search for the most efficient method to translate between English and Spanish in the medical arena. In critical situations that are a daily medical reality, an efficient and practical dictionary created by and for interpreters is an invaluable tool.

Spanish medical terminology is based on Greek and Latin, with an abundance of English cognates. They are easily recognizable for those familiar with medical lexicon. This dictionary aims to be the quick answer to our problems interpreting the remaining words in the most effective way possible, thanks to the inclusion of terminology from various areas of the Spanish-speaking world, allowing the use of words that we already recognize to simplify our professional work.

Francisco Oddone, M.D.
Catholic University of Córdoba, Argentina

INTRODUCTION

Working as a medical interpreter, there was no dictionary that worked for me. Traditional medical dictionaries, with around 50,000 entries, are too voluminous for a mobile interpreter. Modern dictionaries, with around 20,000 entries and flashy titles implying comprehensiveness, have conceded highly technical terminology to portability and to language instruction sections. Yet they still cannot be quickly and discreetly referenced "on the spot" in an interpreting session.

Moreover, newer medical dictionaries are largely targeted to *ad hoc* interpreters. Their basic vocabulary and phonetic exercises are superfluous to the professional interpreter. Translation "apps" are both portable and lexically complete, but are a minefield for mistranslation. Additionally, internet connections and device battery life make them unreliable – and possibly even prohibited in a hospital setting.

Most importantly, all Spanish<>English medical dictionaries are dominated by similar words, or cognates, slowing reference of dissimilar terms as the user fumbles through.

Every medical interpreter occasionally needs a reference tool such as a glossary or dictionary. We specialize in language pairs, not in areas of medicine. Sven Tarp's research for *Lexicographica* notes the lack of specialized bilingual dictionaries, and that specialized translators frequently cannot resolve all of their needs in one dictionary and must employ various tools.

INTRODUCTION

Despite all of the lexicographic tools available, experienced interpreters do not need most of their terminology, since, in the case of English<>Spanish, most are cognates. Cognates were excluded from this dictionary using subjective parameters, mainly degree of recognition to bilingual speakers. A study published in the *The Quarterly Journal of Experimental Psychology* found that for bilinguals, cognates are not morphologically unrelated words subject to translation, but simply variations such as inflections and derivations. Such "variations" as defined are not needed in a dictionary used by a bilingual interpreter. And they slow that interpreter down.

It is not expected that a bilingual knows all the cognates – just that they can be recognized and leveraged. Researchers have documented the mental-linguistic transformation process of translating cognates that is intuitively undertaken by bilingual interpreters, calling it ""Frequency-based Identification of Correct Translation Equivalents (FITE) Obtained through Transformation Rules." In studies thereof, the Spanish<>English recall was especially high. In their academic research entitled "Tapping the Linguistic Resources of Spanish/English Bilinguals: The Role of Cognates in Science," cognates are cited as a "fund of knowledge," and such a fund already exists in the bilingual interpreter's brain.

Any cognate-based strategy must be cognizant of misleading cognates (false cognates or "false friends") on which a section is included herein. For example, "to prescribe" means to order a medication in English, but its cognate "prescribir" means to mandate a method of action, and its actual translation 'recetar" is not a cognate. "Sane" indicates mental health in English, but its cognate "sano" indicates general physical and mental health in Spanish, and its translation "healthy" is not a cognate. "Complexion" translates to "tez" in Spanish, as the Spanish cognate "complexión" means "build" in English.

Building on *Intuitive Interpreting*'s cognate-free dictionary, the glossaries by medical specialty are valuable tools for interpreter preparation. Also abridged to exclude cognates, they are shortlists of terms that an interpreter can review in a few seconds before beginning an interpreting encounter in a given area of medical specialty.

The terminology included is at the register and technical level exhibited in dialogue between a healthcare provider and patient, and not between physicians or healthcare providers with medical expertise. Written by an interpreter, for interpreters, this dictionary serves as a tool to fill the lexical gap that arises when bilinguals interpret intuitively.

Translation is both art and science, and this format employs both, while excluding not only cognates, but also functional labels, inflected forms, and pronunciation. The dictionaries and glossaries in *Intuitive Interpreting* are not complete, and this is by design for "on the job" functionality.

The linguists may furrow their brows, but the interpreter intelligentsia will revel in its efficiency.

INTRODUCTION

HOW TO USE THIS DICTIONARY

Please note that functional labels and cognate word forms are excluded in the interest of brevity and accessibility. The dictionary is targeted to the professional interpreter and purposely incomplete. Reference the introduction for details.

1 ENGLISH-SPANISH DICTIONARY

A

abortion aborto inducido
abrasion raspadura
abruptio placentae desprendimiento prematuro de la placenta
abscess hinchazón
abscess postema
abscess tacotillo
abscess tumorcillo
absent-minded olvidadizo
acetaminophen paracetamol
active ingredient principio activo
acute infarct scintigraphy gammagrama de infarto agudo
acute agudo
Adam's apple nuez de Adán
adhesion adherencia
adipose tissue grasa subcutánea
adrenal gland glándula suprarrenal
Agpar test escala de Agpar
AIDS SIDA
airways vías Pulmiratorias/ aéreas
albuterol salbutamol
amniotic fluid líquido amniótico
ankle tobillo
ankle bone taba
antibodies anticuerpos
antidote contraveneno
antimalarial antipalúdico
antipyretic antifebril
anus ano
anxiety ansiedad
arch support sostén del arco
armpit axila

ASD CIA
athlete's foot pie de atleta
athlete's foot tiña podal
atrial flutter aleteo auricular
atrial septal defect comunicación interauricular
attending (physician) adscrito

B

back brace braguero
back brace espaldera
backbone espinazo
bag of waters fuente
baldness alopecia
ball and socket joint cabeza y cavidad articular
balloon angioplasty angioplastia com sonda balón
bandage envoltura
bandage faja
bandage venda
barachial braquial
barefoot descalzo
beat later
beating paliza
become flushed (to) ruborizarse
bed rest reposo
bedbug chinche
bedpan bacinilla
bedpan orinal
bedridden postrado en cama
belch eructo
belch regueldo

belly   panza, barriga
belt   faja
bend (to)   agacharse
bile   bilis
bile   hiel
biofeedback   biorretroalimentación
biological therapy   bioterapia
bite   mordedura
bite   picadura
bite down (to)   apretar los dientes
blackouts   desmayos
bladder   vejiga
bland diet   régimen de comida no picante
blast cell   hemoblasto
bleeding gums   sangrado de encías
blinking   parpadeo
blister   llaga
blister   ampolla
bloating   hinchazón
blood clot   coágulo de sangre
blood count   biometría hemática
blood culture   hemocultivo
blood presssure cuff   tensiómetro
blood pressure   presión arterial
blood pressure   presión sanguínea
blood pressure cuff   esfigmomanómetro
blood type   grupo sanguíneo
bloodstream   corriente sanguínea
bloody show   desecho con sangre
bloody stool   defecación sanguinolenta
blurred vision   vista nublada
BMI   IMC
body   cuerpo
body (adj)   corporal
body hair   vello
body mass index   índice de masa corporal
boil   absceso
boil   furúnculo
bone infarction   infarto óseo
bone marrow   médula ósea
booster shot   revacunación
booster shot   vacuna de refuerzo
borderline   limítrofe
bottom   nalgas
bowel movement   defecación
bow-legged   chueco
bow-legged   zambo
brace   aparato ortopédico
brain fissure   cisura cerebral
brain scan   imagen del cerebro
brain, cerebrum   cerebro
brains   sesos
brainstem   tallo cerebral

branches   ramas
breast engorgement   atiborramiento de senos
breast feeding, to nurse   amamantar
breast pump   bomba para senos
breast tenderness   mastalgia
breastbone   esternón
breath   respiración
breath (bad)   mal aliento
breech   de nalgas
bronchitis   catarro al pecho
bronchitis   inflamación de los bofes
brow   frente
bruise   morado
bruise   morete
bruise   moretón
buck teeth   dientes salidos
bucket, pail   balde
build   complexión
bulge   prominencia
bump   topetazo
bump (head)   chichón
bundle   haz de his
bunion   juanete
burn (to)   arder
burning sensation   quemazón
burp (to)   repetir
buttocks   trasero
by mouth   por vía bucal
by way of   mediante
bypass   anastomosis quirúrgica
bypass   derivación vascular

C
calf   pantorrilla
callus   callo
cane   bastón
cardiac arrest   paro cardíaco
cardiac output   gasto cardíaco
carpal   carpiana
carpal tunnel syndrome   síndrome de túnel carpiano
cast   yeso
cast (in)   enyesado
CAT scan   tomografía axial computarizada
catheter   sonda
catheter   tubo de drenado
cavity   diente podrido
cavus   cavos
cerebellum   cerebelo
cerebral palsy   parálisis cerebral
cervical cap   capuchón cervical
cervix   cuello del útero

chapped lips labios resecos
charley horse agujeta
chart expediente
cheek mejilla
cheekbone pómulo
chest, breast pecho
chickenpox varicela
chickenpox viruela loca
childbirth parto
chills escalofríos
chills temblorina
chin mentón
chin barbilla
chloasma paño
choke (to) atragantarse
chyme quimo
clammy viscoso
clamp pinza
clamp (finger) broche en el dedo
clearance depuración
cleft lip cucho
cleft lip labio leporino
cleft palate abertura de paladar
cleft palate labio cucho
cleft palate paladar hendido
clinical trial ensayo clínico
clotting coagulación
cloudy urine orina turbia
clubfoot pie torcido
cluster conglomerado
cluster headache cefalea en grupos
coccyx rabadilla
cold sore úlcera en los labios
colic retorcijón
collar bone clavícula
color blind daltónico
coming and going intermitente
complexion tez
compound fracture fractura abierta
compress parche
condition afección
condom preservativo
congenital heart defect cardiopatía
congénita
congestion catarro
charley horse agujeta
chart expediente
cheek mejilla
cheekbone pómulo
chest, breast pecho
chickenpox varicela
chickenpox viruela loca
childbirth parto

chills escalofríos
chills temblorina
chin mentón
chin barbilla
chloasma paño
choke (to) atragantarse
chyme quimo
clammy viscoso
clamp pinza
clamp (finger) broche en el dedo
clearance depuración
cleft lip cucho
cleft lip labio leporino
cleft palate abertura de paladar
cleft palate labio cucho
cleft palate paladar hendido
clinical trial ensayo clínico
clotting coagulación
cloudy urine orina turbia
clubfoot pie torcido
cluster conglomerado
cluster headache cefalea en grupos
coccyx rabadilla
cold sore úlcera en los labios
colic retorcijón
collar bone clavícula
color blind daltónico
coming and going intermitente
complexion tez
compound fracture fractura abierta
compress parche
condition afección
condom preservativo
congenital heart defect cardiopatía
congénita
congestion catarro
congestive heart failutre insuficiencia
cardiaca congestiva
consciousness conocimiento
constipated atrancado(a)
constipation estreñimiento
contact lenses pupilentes
contraceptive anticonceptivo
corner of the eye ángulo del ojo
coronary artery disease arteriopatía
coronaria
coronary heart disease cardiopatía
coronaria
counseling asesoría
counseling consejería
count recuento
counteract contrarrestar
crab louse ladilla

crack trueno
crack (to) tronar
cracked partido
cradle cap costra láctea
cramps calambres
cravings antojos
crib cuna
crick in neck tortícolis
crippled lisiado
crippled tullido
crooked torcido
cross-eyed bizco
cross-eyed estrabismo
cross-eyed turnio
crotch entrepiernas
croup garrotillo
crowning aparición de la cabeza fetal
crush machucar
crushing (pain) aplastante
crutches muletas
CT scan tomografía computarizada
cuff manguito
curettage curetaje
curettage raspado
curl up (to) encogerse
cutterage legrado
cyst quiste

D
D&C dilatación y raspado
dander caspa
dandruff caspa
dark circles under eyes ojeras
dazed atarantado
dazed aturdido
deaf sordo
decongestant descongestivo
deep hondo
deliver (to) dar a luz
delivery expulsión del feto
delivery parto
dental braces frenos dentales
dental floss seda dental
denture dentadura postiza
dentures caja de dientes
dentures prótesis dental
descended prolapso
detached retina desprendimiento de
  retina
detachment desprendimiento
device dispositivo
diaper pañal
diaper rash pañalitis

diaper-urine test (PKU) fenilquetonuria
diarrhea chorrillo
digestive tract tubo digestivo
dimple hoyuelo
disability discapacidad
disability incapacidad
discharge derrame
discharge escurrimiento
discharge (from hospital) dar de alta
discharge, waste desecho
discomfort molestia
disease mal de ...
dislocated zafado
dislocation descoyuntura
dislocation desencaje
dislocation recalcada
dislocation zafadura
disorder trastorno
dizziness tarantas
DNA ADN
DNR órden de no resuscitar
dosage dosificación
dosage posología
dose dosis
douche lavada
Down's syndrome (person) mongólico(a)
dressing vendaje
drool (to) babear
drowsy soñoliento
due date fecha estimada de parto
dull sordo
duodenum duodeno

E
ear plugs tapones de oídos
ear scope otoscopio
eardrum tímpano
early detection detección temprana
earwax cera del oído
effacement of the cervix borramiento del
  cuello
elbow codo
embolism embolio
embryo embrión
end stage etapa terminal
enema laxativa
engorgement ingurgitación
epidemiologic ring cerco epidemiológico
erythrocyte glóbulo rojo
esophagus boca del estómago
estrogen estrógeno
estrogen replacement therapy terapia
  sustitutiva de estrógenos

ethnic group   pertenencia étnica
exhaustion   agotamiento
expectant mother   gestante
expire   vencer
expire air   espirar
eye scope   oftalmoscopio
eyeball   globo del ojo
eyedropper   cuentagotas
eyelid   párpado

F
failure   fallo
faint (to)   desmayarse
faith healer   curandero
fallopian tube   trompa de Falopio
false labor   parto falso
farsighted   hipermétrope
farsighted   hiperópico
fast (food) (to)   ayunar
feces   heces
fertilization, fecundation   fecundación
fester (to)   enconarse
fetal distress   sufrimiento fetal
fetal monitoring   cardiotecografía
fetus   feto
fever blister   fuego
fever blisters   fogazos
fever blisters   llagas de fiebre
fibroid   fibromioma
fibroid   mioma
fibrous tissue   tejido fibroso
fibula   peroné
fill   obturar
fill   surtir
filling   empaste
fingertip   yema del dedo
fist   puño
flabby   blando
flake   escama
flap   colgajo
flare up (to)   agravarse
flatfoot   pie plano
floss   hilo dental
flu   gripe
flushed   sonrojado
followup   control
followup   seguimento
fontanel   mollera
foreskin   prepucio
fracture   quebradura
freckles   pecas
frostbite   congelación
fully aware   plena conciencia

G
gallbladder   vesícula biliar
gallstone   cálculo biliar
gallstones   piedras biliares
ganglion   ganglios
gargle   hacer gárgaras
gash   tajo
gauze   gasa
gender   género
genital warts   condilomas
genital warts   verrugas genitales
germ   germen
germ   microbio
give birth (to)   dar a luz
gland   glándula
glans   glande
goiter   bocio
gonorrhea   purgación
gout   gota
graft   injerto
grate (to)   rechinar
grinding   rozamiento
groin   ingle
guardian   tutor legal
gumline   línea gingival
gums   encías
gunshot   balazo
guts   tripas

H
hairline fracture   fisura
hamstring   tendón de la corva
handicap   minusvalía
hang (to)   ahorcar
hangnail   padrastro
hangnail   uñero
hard nodules   nódulos endurecidos
hard of hearing   medio sordo
hard tumor   cirro
hardening of the arteries   endurecimiento
de las arterias
harelip   labio leporino
hay fever   fiebre de heno
HDL   LAD
headache   cefalea
heal (to)   sanar
healthcare proxy   poder médico
hearing-aid   audífono
heart attack   infarto de miocardio
heart murmur   soplo del corazón
heart rate   frecuencia cardiaca
heartbeat   latido del corazón
heartburn   acidez

heartburn agruras
heating pad cojín eléctrico
heating pad almohadilla eléctrica
heatstroke, sunstroke insolación
heel talón
height gauge talla
height, stature estatura
helplessness impotencia
hematoma moretón
hemorrhoids almorranas
hemorrhoids hemorroides
herida de bala bullet would
hernia rotura
hiccups hipo
hickey chupón
high fiber diet régimen de mucho
residuo
hip cadera
history antecedentes
HIV VIH
HIV antibody test prueba de detección
del VIH
hive roncha
hives or rash urticaria
hoarseness ronquera
Hodgkin's disease linfogranulomatosis
maligna
hold aguantar
hold breath (to) mantener el aire
holder tituar
homeopathic doctor chochero
hookworm anquilostoma
hookworm lombriz de gancho
hookworm nematodo del intestino
hospice centro de cuidados paliativos
hot flashes bochornos
hot flashes calores
hot flashes sofoco

I
IDL LMD
icing aplicación de hielo
incisor colmillo
indigestion empacho
indigestion entripado
ingrown nail uña enterrada
ingrown nail uñero
inhaler inhalador
inherited disorder trastorno heredado
injection, sting piquete
injured lesionado
insole plantilla
instep empeine

insulin pen lapicero de insulina
intrauterine device dispositivo
intrauterino
intravenous pyelogram (IVP) urograma
excretorio
iodine iodo
iodine yodo
itch picazón
itching rascazón
IUD DIU

J
jaundice ictericia
jaw maxilar
jejunum yeyuno
jet injector inyector a chorro
jock itch tiña inguinal
joint articulación
joint coyuntura
joint cavity cavidad articular

K
ketone cetona
kidney riñón
kidney failure insuficiencia renal
kidney stone cálculo renal
kidney stones piedras renales
knee (back) corva
kneecap rótula
kneel (to) hincarse de rodilla
knuckle nudillo

L
labor parto
labor (final) alumbramiento
lacerated cervix cuello desgarrado
large intestine intestino grueso
last rites santos óleos
lateral melleolus maléolo lateral
laxative laxante
laxative purgante
LDL LBD
lead poisoning intoxicación por plomo
lead poisoning saturnismo
lean (to) inclinarse
left-handed zurdo
lens cristalino
leprosy lepra
letdown reflejo del chorro de leche
leukemia leucemia
lice piojo
limp cojear
limp renguear

6

lisping ceceo
little finger dedo meñique
liver hígado
liver failure (severe) insuficiencia hepática grave
load carga
lochia loquios
lock up (to) atorar
locked intestine tripa ida
locked jaw mandíbula desencajada
locked jaw trismo

M

malaria malaria
malaria plaudismo
malnourished desnutrido(a)
malpractice negligencia médica
measles sarampión
mediastinal widening linfodenopatía mediastinal
Medicaid Asistencia Médica del gobierno
medulla tuétano
mental Clinic manicomio
mesh malla
midwife matrona
midwife partera
migraine jaqueca
miocardial infarction infarto del miocardio
miscarriage aborto espontáneo
mite ácaro
MMR triple viral
moan (to) gemir
molar muela
mold hongo
mole lunar
mood disorder trastorno del estado de ánimo
morgue anfiteatro
morgue depósito de cadáveres
morning sickness malestar matutino
MRI imágenes de resonancia magnética
MRI resonancia magnética nuclear
mucous plug tapón mucoso
mucus moco
mumps paperas
mumps parótidas
myoclonic seizure mioclonía

N

nailbed matriz de la uña
narrowed estrechadas
narrowing estenosis

nasal spray atomizador nasal
navel ombligo
nearsighted miope
needle aguja
nerve injury lesiones nerviosas
nervous breakdown crisis nerviosa
nipple (female) pezón
nipple (male) tetilla
nit liendre
nostril fosa nasal
nostril ventanilla
noxious nocivo
nuclear brain scan gammagrama cerebral
numb adormecido
numb entumecido
numbness entumecimiento
nurse practititioner enfermero de pratica avanzada
nursing home ancianato

O

office procedure procedimiento en el consultório
ointment pomada
ointment ungüento
one-arm manco
operating room quirófano
operating table mesa quirúrgica
orthodontic work ortodoncia
orthopedic brace férula para miembros
osteoarthritis artrosis
osteogenic sarcoma osteosarcoma
otolaryngology otorrinolaringología
outpatient, clinic ambulatorio
ovarian cyst quiste ovárico
overdose sobredosis

P

pacemaker marcapasos
pad cojín
painkiller analgésico
painkiller remedio para el dolor
palate paladar
palsy parálisis
pang dolor agudo penetrante
pant (to) jadear
Pap smear citología vaginal
Pap smear prueba de Papanicolau
Pap test examen de Papanicolaou
patch parche
patellofemoral femororrotuliana
patterns patrones
PCP médico de cabecera

peeling of the skin descamación de la piel
perineum periné
perineum perineo
period, menstruation regla
pertussis tos ferina
pharyngitis faringitis
pharynx faringe
phlegm flema
physical therapy fisioterapia
physician's assistant asociado medico
piercing hacerse agujeros en el cuerpo
pimple espinilla
pimple grano
pinch (to) pellizcar
pinkeye conjuntivitis catarral
pinworm gusano pequeño
PKU fenilquetonuria

Q
quadruplet cuatrillizo
quintuplet quintillizo

R
radiocarpal radiocarpiana
radiolunar radiocubital
raise (to) alzar
rash erupción cutánea
rash sarpullido
rash and swelling pasmo
rebound rebote
rectal exam tacto rectal
rectum recto
red blood cell eritrocito
red blood cell glóbulo rojo
relapse recaída
remove (to) extirpar
renal failure insuficiencia renal
resident médico en capacitación
resting pulse pulso en reposo
restlessness desasosiego
restlessness inquietud
restorative reparador
resuscitation reanimación
rheumatism riuma
rib costilla
rib cage caja torácica
rickets raquitismo
ringing in ears zumbido en los oídos
ringworm tiña
ringworm tiña
rinse (to) enjuagar
roof of mouth paladar
root canal canal en la raíz

root canal conducto radicular
root canal tratamiento de conductos
rotator cuff rotador del hombro
rubella rubeola
ruido bruit
ruptured roto
ruptured disk disco roto

S
sacrum rabadilla
safety pins ganchos
saliva baba
sanitary pads toallas
scab costra
scabies escabiosis
scabies sarna
scale báscula
scale balanza
scalp cuero cabelludo
scalpel bisturí
scan imagen diagnóstica
scar cicatriz
scar tissue tejido cicatrizal
SCD muerte cardiaca repentina
sclera esclerótica
scrapings raspaduras
scratch (to) rasguñar
screen examen de detección
screening detección sistemática
sed rate (erythrocyte sedimentation rate) velocidade de sedimentación globular
sedative calmante
seizure ataque
sense of smell sentido de olfato
septum tabique
serum suero
shaft mango
shake (to) agitar
sharp afilado
sharp agudo
sheath vaina
shelter asilo
shin canilla
shin tibia
shingles culebrilla
shingles herpes zoster
shock therapy terapia electroconvulsiva
shortness of breath ahogo
shortness of breath disnea
shoulder blade omóplato
sickle cell anemia anemia de glóbulos falciformes

side effect reacción adversa
side stitch ijada
sinus seno
sitz bath baño de asiento
skin cutis
skull cráneo
skull calavera
sleepwalking sonambulismo
sliding scale escala móvil
sling cabestrillo
sling honda
slippage estiramento
slipped disk disco desplazado
slipped disk disco zafado
small intestine intestino delgado
smallpox viruela
smallpox vaccine vacuna antivariólica
smear frotis
sneeze (to) estornudar
snore (to) roncar
sober sobrio
socket cavidad
socket cuenca
sonogram ecografía
sore (open) llaga abierta
speculum espéculo
speech difficulties trastornos del habla
spell ataque de
sphincter esfinter
sphygmomanometer baumanómetro
spinal column columna vertebral
spinal cord médula espinal
spinal tap drenaje espinal
spinal tap punción lumbar
spine espina dorsal
spine espina vertebral
spirometer espirómetro
spit (up) (to) escupir
spleen bazo
splint férula
splint tablilla
spotting manchas de flujo vaginal con
  sangre
spotting sangrado ligero
sprain esguince
sprain falseado
sprain torcedura
spread (to) diseminarse
spread (to) propagarse
spur espolón
spur esquince
sputum esputo
squat (to) acuclillarse

squat (to) ponerse en cuclillas
squeeze estrujar
squint (to) fruncir
squint (to) mirar entecerrado
stab wound cuchillada
stabbing picante
standby pacemaker marcapasos de
  demanda
staple grapa
sternum esternón
stethescope estetoscopio
stiff tieso
stiff neck cuello rígido
stillbirth nacimiento de bebé muerto
stillborn nacido muerto
stirrup estribo
stitches suturas
stitches puntos
stomach vientre
stomach cramp retorcijón
stomach gas pedos
stone cálculo
stool culture coprocultivo
straight cane bordón
streaks rayas
stress esfuerzo
stress test prueba de esfuerzo
stretch tramo
stretch mark estría
stretcher camilla
strips tiras
stroke apoplejía
stroke derrame cerebral
stroke embolia
stuffy nose nariz tapada
stuttering tartamudeo
sty orzuelo
subtalar subastragalina
suction succión
suction curettage aspiración com vacío
sudden súbito
sunscreen pantalla solar
suppository calía
suppository óvulo
surgeon cirujano(a)
surgical needle aguja para suturas
surveillance vigilancia
swab hisopo
sweat glands glándulas sudoríparas
sweats sudores
swelling, inflammation, puffiness
  hinchazón
swollen hinchado

symptom padecimiento
symptom seña
syringe jeringa
systemic weakness achaque

T
tailbone cóccix
tailbone colita
talofibular ligament ligamento peroneoastragalino
talus astrágalo
tangles marañas
tapeworm solitaria
tapeworm tenia
tartar sarro
taste (sense) gusto
taste buds papilas gustativas
tear desgarre
tear a ligament desgarrar um ligamento
tear duct conduto lacrimal
temple sien
temporal mandibular joint (TMJ) articulación temporomandibular
tetanus tétano
tetanus (shot) antitetánica
thalamus tálamo
thickening engrosamiento
thigh muslo
thinner diluyente
thorax tronco
threadworm oxiuros
threshhold umbral
throb (to) palpitar
throbbing punzante
thump porrazo
thymus timo
thyroid tiroides
tick garrapata
tight chest tensión en el pecho
tingle hormiguear
tissues tejidos
tongue depressor abate lengua
tongue depressor bajalenguas
tonsillitis amigdalitis
tonsils agallas
tonsils amígdalas
tooth decay caries dental
toothache dolor de muela
torn ligament desgarramiento
torn ligament esguince
touch (sense) tacto
tracing trazo
tranquilizer calmante

triggers accionadores
triggers irritantes
triggers provocadores
triplet trillizo
tubal ligation ligadura de trompas/ tubos
tubal pregnancy embarazo tubárico
tube conducto
tube trompa
tumor incordio
tweezers pinzas
twin (fraternal) cuate
twin (fraternal) mellizo
twin (identical) gemelo
twitch contracción espasmódica
twitch contorsión
twitch (to) crisparse

U
ultrasound ecografía
umbilical band ombliguero
upper GI tubo digestivo superior
upset revuelto
ureter caño de la orina
urethroscope fibroscopio urinario

V
vaccine vacuna
varicose veins várices
varicose veins venas varicosas
vas deferens conducto deferente
vein stripping extracción de várices
venipuncture venopunción
ventilator Pulmirador
ventrical septal defect comunicación interventricular
vertigo vahído
viral load testing prueba de carga viral
vision chart cuadro de agudeza visual

W
wart verruga
wean (to) destetar
wheeze chillarle el pecho
wheeze silbido
wheezing sibilancias
wheezing Pulmiración sibilante/ silbante
whiplash desnucamiento
whistling chiflido
white blood cell glóbulo blanco
white blood cell leucocito
whooping cough tos ferina
windpipe gaznate
withdrawal abstinencia

withdrawal privación
withdrawal symptoms síntomas de
  desintoxicación
womb matriz
work release relevo de trabajo
worthlessness inutilidad
wrist muñeca

X
x-rays rayos equis

Y
yawn (to) bostezar
yeast hongos
yeast infection hongos vaginales
yeast infection micosis vaginal

Z
zit grano

ENGLISH-SPANISH DICTIONARY

2 SPANISH-ENGLISH DICTIONARY

A

abate lengua tongue depressor
abertura de paladar cleft palate
aborto espontáneo miscarriage
aborto inducido abortion
absceso boil
abstinencia withdrawal
abultamiento lump
ácaro mite
accionadores triggers
achaque systemic weakness
acidez heartburn
acuclillarse squat (to)
adherencia adhesion
ADN DNA
adormecido numb
adscrito attending (physician)
afección condition
afilado sharp
agacharse bend (to)
agallas tonsils
agitar shake (to)
agotamiento exhaustion
agravarse flare up (to)
agrietado chapped
agruras heartburn
aguantar hold
agudo acute
agudo sharp
aguja needle
aguja para suturas surgical needle

agujeta charley horse
ahogo shortness of breath
ahorcar hang (to)
aleteo auricular atrial flutter
aliento (mal) breath (bad)
almohadilla eléctrica heating pad
almorranas hemorrhoids
alopecia baldness
alumbramiento labor (final)
alzar raise (to)
amamantar breast feeding, to nurse
ambulatorio outpatient, clinic
amígdalas tonsils
amigdalitis tonsillitis
ampolla blister
analgésico painkiller
anastomosis quirúrgica bypass
ancianato nursing home
anemia de glóbulos falciformes sickle cell anemia
anfiteatro morgue
angioplastia com sonda balón balloon angioplasty
ángulo del ojo corner of the eye
ano anus
anquilostoma hookworm
ansiedad anxiety
antecedentes history
antes del parto prelabor
anticonceptivo contraceptive

13

anticuerpo antibody
anticuerpos antibodies
antifebril antipyretic
antipalúdico antimalarial
antitetánica tetanus (shot)
antojos cravings
aparato ortopédico brace
aparición de la cabeza fetal crowning
aplastante crushing (pain)
apoplejía stroke
apretar los dientes bite down (to)
arder burn (to)
arteriopatía coronaria coronary artery disease
articulación joint
articulación temporomandibular temporal mandibular joint (TMJ)
artrosis osteoarthritis
asesoría counseling
asilo shelter
Asistencia Médica del Gobierno Medicaid
asociado medico physician's assistant
aspiración com vacío suction curettage
astrágalo talus
ataque seizure
ataque de spell
atarantado dazed
atiborramiento de senos breast engorgement
atomizador nasal nasal spray
atorar lock up (to)
atragantarse choke (to)
atrancado(a) constipated
aturdido dazed
audífono hearing-aid
axila axilla, armpit
ayunar fast (food) (to)

B
baba saliva
babear drool (to)
bacinilla bedpan
bajalenguas tongue depressor
balanza scale
balazo gunshot
balde bucket, pail
baño de asiento sitz bath
barbilla chin
barriga belly
báscula scale

bastón cane
baumanómetro sphygmomanometer
bazo spleen
bilis bile
biometría hemática blood count
biorretroalimentación biofeedback
bioterapia biological therapy
bisturí scalpel
bizco cross-eyed
boca del estómago esophagus
bochornos hot flashes
bocio goiter
bomba pump
bomba para senos breast pump
bordón straight cane
borramiento del cuello effacement of the cervix
bostezar yawn (to)
braguero back brace
braquial barachial
broche en el dedo clamp (finger)
bruit ruido
bullet would herida de bala
bulto lump

C
cabestrillo sling
cabeza y cavidad articular ball and socket joint
cadera hip
caída de la matriz prolapse of the uterus
caja de dientes dentures
caja torácica rib cage
calambres cramps
calavera skull
cálculo stone
cálculo biliar gallstone
cálculo renal kidney stone
calía suppository
callo callus
calmante tranquilizer, sedative
calores hot flashes
camilla stretcher
canal en la raíz root canal
canilla shin
caño de la orina ureter
capuchón cervical cervical cap
cardiopatía congénita congenital heart defect
cardiopatía coronaria coronary heart disease
cardiotecografía fetal monitoring
carga load

caries dental   tooth decay
carpiana   carpal
caspa   dander
caspa   dandruff
catarro   congestion
catarro al pecho   bronchitis
cavidad   socket
cavidad articular   joint cavity
cavos   cavus
ceceo   lisping
cefalea   headache
cefalea en grupos   cluster headache
centro de cuidados paliativos   hospice
cera del oído   earwax
cerco epidemiológico   epidemiologic ring
cerebelo   cerebellum
cerebro   brain, cerebrum
cetona   ketone
CIA   ASD
cicatriz   scar
cirro   hard tumor
cirujano(a)   surgeon
cisura cerebral   brain fissure
citología vaginal   pap smear
clavícula   collar bone
coagulación   clotting
coágulo de sangre   blood clot
cóccix   tailbone
codo   elbow
cojear   limp
cojín eléctrico   heating pad
colgajo   flap
colita   tailbone
colmillo   incisor
columna vertebral   spinal column
complexión   build
comunicación interauricular   atrial septal
   defect
comunicación interventricular   ventrical
septal defect
condilomas   genital warts
conducto   tube
conducto deferente   vas deferens
conducto radicular   root canal
conduto lacrimal   tear duct
congelación   frostbite
conglomerado   cluster
conocimiento   consciousness
consejería   counseling
contorsión   twitch
contracción espasmódica   twitch
contrarrestar   counteract
control   followup

coprocultivo   stool culture
corporal   body (adj)
corriente sanguínea   bloodstream
corva   back of knee
costilla   rib
costra   scab
costra láctea   cradle cap
coyuntura   joint
cráneo   skull
crisis nerviosa   nervous breakdown
crisparse   twitch (to)
cristalino   lens
crujido   popping
cuadro de agudeza visual   vision chart
cuate   twin (fraternal)
cuatrillizo   quadruplet
cuchillada   stab wound
cucho   cleft lip
cuello del útero   cervix
cuello desgarrado   lacerated cervix
cuello rígido   stiff neck
cuenca   socket
cuentagotas   eyedropper
cuero cabelludo   scalp
cuerpo   body
culebrilla   shingles
cuna   crib
curetaje   curettage
cutis   skin

CH
chichón   bump (head)
chiflido   whistling
chillarle el pecho   wheeze
chinche   bedbug
chochero   homeopathic doctor
chorrillo   diarrhea
chueco   bow-legged
chupón   hickey

D
daltónico   color blind
dar a luz   deliver (to)
dar a luz   give birth (to)
dar de alta   discharge (from hospital)
de nalgas   breech
dedo meñique   little finger
defecación   bowel movement
defecación sanguinolenta   bloody stool
dentadura postiza   denture
depósito de cadáveres   morgue
depuración   clearance
derivación vascular   bypass

derrame discharge
derrame cerebral stroke
desasosiego restlessness
descamación de la piel peeling of the skin
descongestivo decongestant
descoyuntura dislocation
desecho discharge, waste
desecho con sangre bloody show
desencaje dislocation
desgarramiento torn ligament
desgarrar um ligamento tear a ligament
desgarre tear
desmayarse faint (to)
desmayos blackouts
desnucamiento whiplash
desnutrido(a) malnourished
desprendimiento detachment
desprendimiento de retina detached retina
desprendimiento prematuro de la placenta abruptio placentae
destetar wean (to)
detección sistemática screening
detección temprana early detection
diente podrido cavity
dientes salidos buck teeth
dieta hiposódica low sodium diet
dilatación y raspado D&C
diluyente thinner
discapacidad disability
disco desplazado slipped disk
disco roto ruptured disk
disco zafado slipped disk
diseminarse spread (to)
disnea shortness of breath
dispositivo device
dispositivo intrauterino intrauterine device
DIU IUD
dolor de muela toothache
dosificación dosage
dosis dose
drenaje espinal spinal tap
duodeno duodenum

E
ecografía sonogram
ecografía ultrasound
embarazo tubárico tubal pregnancy
embolia stroke
embolio embolism
embrión embryo

empacho indigestion
empaste filling
empeine instep
encías gums
encogerse curl up (to)
enconarse fester (to)
endurecimiento de las arterias hardening of the arteries
enfermero de pratica avanzada nurse practititioner
engrosamiento thickening
enjuagar rinse (to)
ensayo clínico clinical trial
entrepiernas crotch
entripado indigestion
entumecido numb
entumecimiento numbness
envoltura bandage
enyesado in a cast
eructo belch
erupción cutánea rash
escabiosis scabies
escala de Agpar Agpar test
escala móvil sliding scale
escalofríos chills
escama flake
escara burn scab
esclerótica sclera
escupir spit (up) (to)
escurrimiento discharge
esfigmomanómetro blood pressure cuff
esfinter sphincter
esfuerzo stress
esguince sprain
esguince torn ligament
espaldera back brace
espéculo speculum
espina dorsal spine
espina vertebral spine
espinazo backbone
espinilla pimple
espirar expire air
espirómetro spirometer
espolón spur
esputo sputum
esquince spur
estatura height, stature
esternón breastbone
esternón sternum
estetoscopio stethescope
estiramento slippage
estornudar sneeze (to)
estrabismo cross-eyed

estreñimiento constipation
estría stretch mark
estribo stirrup
estrógeno estrogen
estrujar squeeze
etapa terminal end stage
examen de detección screen
examen de Papanicolaou Pap test
expediente chart
expulsión del feto delivery
extirpar remove (to)
extracción de várices vein stripping

F
faja bandage
faja belt
fallo failure
falseado sprain
faringe pharynx
faringitis pharyngitis
fecha estimada de parto due date
fecundación fertilization, fecundation
femororrotuliana patellofemoral
fenilquetonuria diaper-urine test (PKU)
fenilquetonuria PKU
férula splint
férula para miembros orthopedic brace
feto fetus
fibromioma fibroid
fibroscopio urinario urethroscope
fiebre de heno hay fever
fisioterapia physical therapy
fisura hairline fracture
flema phlegm
fogazos fever blisters
fosa nasal nostril
fractura abierta compound fracture
frecuencia cardiaca heart rate
frenos dentales dental braces
frente brow
frotis smear
fruncir squint (to)
fuego fever blister

G
gammagrama cerebral nuclear brain scan
gammagrama de infarto agudo acute
infarct scintigraphy
ganchos safety pins
ganglio linfático lymph node
ganglios ganglion
garrapata tick
garrotillo croup

gasa gauze
gasto cardíaco cardiac output
gaznate windpipe
gemelo twin (identical
gemir moan (to)
género gender
germen germ
gestante expectant mother
glande glans
glándula gland
glándula suprarrenal adrenal gland
glándulas sudoríparas sweat glands
globo del ojo eyeball
glóbulo blanco white blood cell
glóbulo rojo erythrocyte
glóbulo rojo red blood cell
gota gout
grano pimple
grapa staple
grasa subcutánea adipose tissue
gripe flu
grupo sanguíneo blood type
gusano pequeño pinworm
gusto taste (sense)

H
hacer gárgaras gargle
hacerse agujeros en el cuerpo piercing
haz de his bundle
hemoblasto blast cell
hemocultivo blood culture
hemorroides hemorrhoids
herpes zoster shingles
hiel bile
hígado liver
hilo dental floss
hincarse de rodilla kneel (to)
hinchado swollen, bloated
hinchazón abscess
hinchazón bloating
hinchazón swelling, inflammation,
  puffiness
hipermétrope farsighted
hipo hiccups
hisopo swab
honda sling
hondo deep
hongo mold
hongos yeast
hongos en los pies athlete's foot
hongos vaginales yeast infection
hormiguear tingle
hoyo de la nariz nasal cavity

hoyuelo dimple

I
ictericia jaundice
ijada side stitch
imagen del cerebro brain scan
imagen diagnóstica scan
imágenes de resonancia magnética MRI
IMC BMI
impotencia helplessness
incapacidad disability
inclinarse lean (to)
incordio tumor
índice de masa corporal body mass index
inflamación de los bofes bronchitis
infarto de miocardio heart attack
infarto del miocardio miocardial
 infarction
infarto óseo bone infarction
inflamación puffiness
infusor infuser
ingle groin
ingurgitación engorgement
inhalador inhaler
injerto graft
inquietud restlessness
insolación heatstroke, sunstroke
insuficiencia cardiaca congestiva
 congestive heart failutre
insuficiencia hepática grave severe liver
 failure
insuficiencia renal kidney failure
insuficiencia renal renal failure
intermitente coming and going
intestino delgado small intestine
intestino grueso large intestine
intoxicación por plomo lead poisoning
intoxicado poisoned
inutilidad worthlessness
inyector a chorro jet injector
iodo iodine
irritantes triggers

J
jadear pant (to)
jaqueca migraine
jeringa syringe
juanete bunion

L
labio cucho cleft palate
labio leporino cleft lip
labio leporino harelip

labios resecos chapped lips
LAD HDL
ladilla crab louse
lapicero de insulina insulin pen
later beat
latido del corazón heartbeat
lavada douche
laxante laxative
laxativa enema
lazo loop
LBD LDL
legrado cutterage
lepra leprosy
lesionado injured
lesiones nerviosas nerve injury
leucemia leukemia
leucocito white blood cell
liendre nit
ligadura de trompas/ tubos tubal
 ligation
ligamento peroneoastragalino talofibular
 ligament
limítrofe borderline
línea gingival gumline
linfa lymph
linfocito lymphocyte
linfodenopatía mediastinal mediastinal
 widening
linfogranulomatosis maligna Hodgkin's
 disease
líquido amniótico amniotic fluid
lisiado crippled
LMD IDL
lombriz de gancho hookworm
loquios lochia
lunar mole

LL
llaga blister
llaga abierta sore (open)
llagas de fiebre fever blisters

M
machucar crush
mal aliento bad breath
mal de ... disease
malaria malaria
maléolo lateral lateral melleolus
malestar matutino morning sickness
malla mesh
manchas de flujo vaginal con sangre
 spotting
manco one-arm

mandíbula desencajada   locked jaw
mango   shaft
manguito   cuff
manicomio   mental Clinic
mantener el aire   hold breath (to)
marañas   tangles
marcapasos   pacemaker
marcapasos de demanda   standby
  pacemaker
mastalgia   breast tenderness
matriz   womb
matrona   midwife
maxilar   jaw
mediante   by way of
médico de cabecera   PCP
médico en capacitación   resident
medio sordo   hard of hearing
médula espinal   spinal cord
médula ósea   bone marrow
mejilla   cheek
mellizo   twin (fraternal)
mentón   chin
mesa quirúrgica   operating table
micosis vaginal   yeast infection
microbio   germ
minusvalía   handicap
mioclonía   myoclonic seizure
mioma   fibroid
miope   nearsighted
mirar entecerrado   squint (to)
moco   mucus
molestia   discomfort
mollera   fontanel
mongólico(a)   Down's syndrome (person)
morado   bruise
mordedura   bite
morete   bruise
moretón   bruise
moretón   hematoma
muela   molar
muerte cardiaca repentina   SCD
muletas   crutches
muñeca   wrist
muslo   thigh

N
nacido muerto   stillborn
nacimiento de bebé muerto   stillbirth
nalgas   bottom
nariz tapada   stuffy nose
negligencia médica   malpractice
nematodo del intestino   hookworm
neumólogo   pulmonologist

nocivo   noxious
nódulo linfático   lymph node
nódulos endurecidos   hard nodules
nuca   nape
nudillo   knuckle
nuez de Adán   Adam's apple

O
obturar   fill
oftalmoscopio   eye scope
ojeras   dark circles under eyes
olvidadizo   absent-minded
ombligo   navel
ombliguero   umbilical band
omóplato   shoulder blade
órden de no resuscitar   DNR
orina turbia   cloudy urine
orinal   bedpan
ortodoncia   orthodontic work
orzuelo   sty
osteosarcoma   osteogenic sarcoma
otorrinolaringología   otolaryngology
otoscopio   ear scope
óvulo   suppository
oxiuros   threadworm

P
padecimiento   symptom
padrastro   hangnail
paladar   palate
paladar   roof of mouth
paladar hendido   cleft palate
paliza   beating
palpitar   throb (to)
pañal   diaper
pañalitis   diaper rash
paño   chloasma
pantalla solar   sunscreen
pantorrilla   calf
panza   belly
paperas   mumps
papilas gustativas   taste buds
paracetamol   acetaminophen
parálisis   palsy
parálisis cerebral   cerebral palsy
parche   compress
parche   patch
paro cardíaco   cardiac arrest
parótidas   mumps
parpadeo   blinking
párpado   eyelid
partera   midwife
partido   cracked

parto delivery
parto labor
parto childbirth
parto falso false labor
pasmo rash and swelling
patrones patterns
pecas freckles
pecho chest, breast
pedos stomach gas
pellizcar pinch (to)
periné perineum
perineo perineum
peroné fibula
pertenencia étnica ethnic group
peste plague
pezón nipple (female)
picadura bite
picante stabbing
picazón itch
pie de atleta athlete's foot
pie plano flatfoot
pie torcido clubfoot
piedras biliares gallstones
piedras renales kidney stones
pinchar prick (to)
pinchazo prick
pinza clamp
pinzas tweezers
piojo lice
piojo del pubis pubic lice
pibquete injection, sting
plantilla insole
plaqueta platelet
plaudismo malaria
plena conciencia fully aware
poder médico healthcare proxy
pólipo polyp
póliza policy
pomada ointment
pómulo cheekbone
ponerse en cuclillas squat (to)
por vía bucal by mouth
porrazo thump
posología dosage
postema abscess
postrado en cama bedridden
prepucio foreskin
pre-qrúrguiica pre-op
preservativo condom
presión arterial blood pressure
presión sanguínea blood pressure
principio activo active ingredient
privación withdrawal

probeta probe
procedimiento en el consultório office
  procedure
prolapso descended
prominencia bulge
propagarse spread (to)
prótesis dental dentures
protuberancia lump
provocadores triggers
prueba de carga viral viral load testing
prueba de detección del VIH HIV
  antibody test
prueba de esfuerzo stress test
prueba de Papanicolau pap smear
pubertad puberty
pubis pubic area
pulmiración sibilante/ silbante
  wheezing
pulmirador ventilator
pulmón lung
pulso en reposo resting pulse
punción lumbar spinal tap
puño fist
puntos stitches
punzada puncture
punzante throbbing
pupilentes contact lenses
purgación gonorrhea
purgante laxative

Q

quebradura fracture
quemazón burning sensation
quimo chyme
quintillizo quintuplet
quirófano operating room
quiste cyst
quiste ovárico ovarian cyst

R

rabadilla coccyx
rabadilla sacrum
radiocarpiana radiocarpal
radiocubital radiolunar
ramas branches
raquitismo rickets
rascazón itching
rasguñar scratch (to)
raspado curettage
raspadura abrasion
raspaduras scrapings
rayas streaks
reacción adversa side effect

reanimación resuscitation
rebote rebound
recaída relapse
recalcada dislocation
receta médica prescription
rechinar grate (to)
recto rectum
recuento count
reflejo del chorro de leche letdown
régimen de comida no picante bland diet
régimen de mucho residuo high fiber diet
regla period, menstruation
regueldo belch
relevo de trabajo work release
renguear limp
reparador restorative
repetir burp (to)
reposo bed rest
resonancia magnética nuclear MRI
respiración breath
retorcijón colic
retorcijón stomach cramp
revacunación booster shot
revuelto upset
riñón kidney
riuma rheumatism
roble venenoso poison oak
roncar snore (to)
roncha hive
ronquera hoarseness
rotador del hombro rotator cuff
roto ruptured
rótula kneecap
rotura hernia
rozamiento grinding
rubeola rubella
ruborizarse become flushed (to)

S
salbutamol albuterol
sanar heal (to)
sangrado de encías bleeding gums
sangrado ligero spotting
santos óleos last rites
sarampión measles
sarna scabies
sarpullido rash
sarro tartar
saturnismo lead poisoning
seda dental dental floss
sedante sedative, tranquilizer

seguimento followup
semilunar lunate
seña symptom
seno sinus
sentido de olfato sense of smell
sesos brains
sibilancias wheezing
SIDA AIDS
sien temple
silbido wheeze
síndrome de túnel carpiano carpal tunnel syndrome
síntomas de desintoxicación withdrawal symptoms
sobredosis overdose
sobrio sober
sofoco hot flashes
solitaria tapeworm
sonambulismo sleepwalking
sonda catheter
soñoliento drowsy
sonrojado flushed
soplo del corazón heart murmur
sordo deaf
sordo dull
sostén del arco arch support
subastragalina subtalar
súbito sudden
succión suction
sudores sweats
suero serum
sufrimiento fetal fetal distress
surtir fill
suturas stitches

T
taba ankle bone
tabique septum
tablilla splint
tacotillo abscess
tacto touch (sense)
tacto rectal rectal exam
tajo gash
tálamo thalamus
talla height gauge
tallo cerebral brainstem
talón heel
tapón mucoso mucous plug
tapones de oídos ear plugs
tarantas dizziness
tartamudeo stuttering
tejido cicatrizal scar tissue
tejido fibroso fibrous tissue

tejidos tissues
temblorina chills
tendón de la corva hamstring
tenia tapeworm
tensiómetro blood presssure cuff
tensión en el pecho chest tightness
terapia sustitutiva de estrógenos
  estrogen replacement therapy
terapia electroconvulsiva shock
  therapy
tétano tetanus
tetilla nipple (male)
tez complexion
tibia shin
tieso stiff
timo thymus
tímpano eardrum
tiña ringworm
tiña ringworm
tiña inguinal jock itch
tiña podal athlete's foot
tiras strips
tiroides thyroid
tirón pulled muscle
tituar holder
toallas sanitary pads
tobillo ankle
tomografía axial computarizada CAT
  scan
tomografía computarizada CT scan
topetazo bump
torcedura sprain
torcido crooked
tortícolis crick in neck
tos ferina pertussis
tos ferina whooping cough
tramo stretch
trasero buttocks
trastorno disorder
trastorno del estado de ánimo mood
  disorder
trastorno heredado inherited disorder
trastornos del habla speech difficulties
tratamiento de conductos root canal
trazo tracing
trillizo triplet
tripa ida locked intestine
tripas guts
triple viral MMR
trismo locked jaw
trompa tube
trompa de falopio fallopian tube
tronar crack (to)

tronco thorax
trueno crack
tubo de drenado catheter
tubo digestivo superior upper GI
tuétano medulla
tullido crippled
tumorcillo abscess
tumorectomía lumpectomy
turnio cross-eyed
tutor legal guardian

U
úlcera en los labios cold sore
umbral threshhold
uña enterrada ingrown nail
uñero hangnail
uñero ingrown nail
ungüento ointment
urograma excretorio intravenous
  pyelogram (IVP)
urticaria hives or rash

V
vacuna vaccine
vacuna antivariólica smallpox vaccine
vacuna de refuerzo booster shot
vahído vertigo
vaina sheath
varicela chickenpox
várices varicose veins
vejiga bladder
vello body hair
vello púbico pubic hair
velocidade de sedimentación globular
  sed rate (erythrocyte sedimentation rate)
venas varicosas varicose veins
vencer expire
vendaje dressing
venopunción venipuncture
ventanilla nostril
verruga wart
verrugas genitales genital warts
vesícula biliar gallbladder

Y
yema del dedo fingertip
yeso cast
yeyuno jejunum
yodo iodine

Z
zafado dislocated
zafadura dislocation

zambo bow-legged
zumbido en los oídos ringing in ears
zurdo left-handed

3 GLOSSARIES BY MEDICAL SPECIALTY AND BY CONCEPT

ENGLISH-SPANISH, SPANISH-ENGLISH

ANATOMY
CARDIOLOGY
CLINICAL
DENTISTRY
DERMATOLOGY
EAR, NOSE, & THROAT (Otolaryngology)
GASTROENTEROLOGY AND UROLOGY
IMMUNOLOGY AND INFECTIOUS DISEASE
LABORATORY AND HEMATOLOGY
NEPHROLOGY AND ENDICRINOLOGY
NEUROLOGY
OBSTETRICS AND GYNECOLOGY
ONCOLOGY
OPHTHALMOLOGY
ORTHOPEDICS
PEDIATRICS
PHARMACY
PSYCHOLOGY
PULMONOLOGY
SYMPTOMS
UROLOGY

ANATOMY

Adam's apple   nuez de Adán
adipose tissue   grasa subcutánea
adrenal gland   glándula suprarrenal
airways   vías pulmiratorias/ aéreas
ankle bone   taba
anus   ano
axilla, armpit   axila
back of knee   corva
backbone   espinazo
ball and socket joint   cabeza y cavidad
   articular
belly   barriga
belly   panza
bladder   vejiga
body   cuerpo
bottom   nalgas
brain, cerebrum   cerebro
brainstem   tallo cerebral
breastbone   esternón
brow   frente
buttocks   trasero
calf   pantorrilla
cerebellum   cerebelo
cervical cap   capuchón cervical
cervix   cuello del útero
cheek   mejilla
cheekbone   pómulo
chest, breast   pecho
chin   mentón
chin   barbilla
coccyx, sacrum   rabadilla
collar bone   clavícula
corner of the eye   ángulo del ojo
crotch   entrepiernas
duodenum   duodeno
elbow   codo
esophagus   boca del estómago
eyeball   globo del ojo
eyelid   párpado
fibrous tissue   tejido fibroso
fibula   peroné
fist   puño
foreskin   prepucio
gallbladder   vesícula biliar
gland   glándula
glans   glande
groin   ingle
gumline   línea gingival
gums   encías
hamstring   tendón de la corva
hard nodules   nódulos endurecidos

heel   talón
insole   plantilla
jaw   maxilar
joint   articulación
joint   coyuntura
joint cavity   cavidad articular
kneecap   rótula
knuckle   nudillo
lateral melleolus   maléolo lateral
little finger   dedo meñique
liver   hígado
lochia   loquios
lung   pulmón
lymph   linfa
lymph node   ganglio linfático
lymph node   nódulo linfático
lymph node   nódulo linfático
nape   nuca
navel   ombligo
nipple (female)   pezón
nipple (male)   tetilla
nostril   fosa nasal
nostril   ventanilla
palate   paladar
perineum   periné
perineum   perineo
pubic area   pubis
rib cage   caja torácica
roof of mouth   paladar
rotator cuff   rotador del hombro
septum   tabique
shin   canilla
shin   tibia
shoulder blade   omóplato
skull   cráneo
skull   calavera
socket   cavidad
sphincter   esfinter
spinal column   columna vertebral
spinal cord   médula espinal
spine   espina dorsal
spine   espina vertebral
spleen   bazo
stomach   vientre
subtalar   subastragalina
sweat glands   glándulas sudoríparas
tailbone   cóccix
tailbone   colita
talofibular ligament   ligamento
   peroneoastragalino
talus   astrágalo

tear duct   conduto lacrimal
temple   sien
thalamus   tálamo
thigh   muslo
thorax   tronco
thymus   timo
thyroid   tiroides
tissues   tejidos
tonsils   agallas
tonsils   amígdalas
tube   trompa
upper GI   tubo digestivo superior
ureter   caño de la orina
vas deferens   conducto deferente
windpipe   gaznate
womb   matriz
wrist   muñeca

ANATOMÍA

agallas tonsils
amígdalas tonsils
ángulo del ojo corner of the eye
ano anus
articulación joint
astrágalo talus
axila axilla, armpit
barbilla chin
barriga belly
bazo spleen
boca del estómago esophagus
cabeza y cavidad articular ball and
  socket joint
caja torácica rib cage
calavera skull
canilla shin
caño de la orina ureter
capuchón cervical cervical cap
cavidad socket
cavidad articular joint cavity
cerebelo cerebellum
cerebro brain, cerebrum
clavícula collar bone
cóccix tailbone
codo elbow
colita tailbone
columna vertebral spinal column
conducto deferente vas deferens
conduto lacrimal tear duct
corva back of knee
coyuntura joint
cráneo skull
cuello del útero cervix
cuerpo body
dedo meñique little finger
duodeno duodenum
encias gums
entrepiernas crotch
esfinter sphincter
espina dorsal spine
espina vertebral spine
espinazo backbone
esternón breastbone
fosa nasal nostril
frente brow
ganglio linfático lymph node
gaznate windpipe
glande glans
glándula gland
glándula suprarrenal adrenal gland

glándulas sudoríparas sweat glands
globo del ojo eyeball
grasa subcutánea adipose tissue
hígado liver
ingle groin
ligamento peroneoastragalino talofibular
ligament
linea gingival gumline
linfa lymph
loquios lochia
maléolo lateral lateral melleolus
matriz womb
maxilar jaw
médula espinal spinal cord
mejilla cheek
mentón chin
muñeca wrist
muslo thigh
nalgas bottom
nódulo linfático lymph node
nódulo linfático lymph node
nódulos endurecidos hard nodules
nuca nape
nudillo knuckle
nuez de Adán Adam's apple
ombligo navel
omóplato shoulder blade
paladar palate
paladar roof of mouth
pantorrilla calf
panza belly
párpado eyelid
pecho chest, breast
periné perineum
perineo perineum
peroné fibula
pezón nipple (female)
plantilla insole
pómulo cheekbone
prepucio foreskin
pubis pubic area
pulmón lung
puño fist
rabadilla coccyx, sacrum
rotador del hombro rotator cuff
rótula kneecap
sien temple
subastragalina subtalar
taba ankle bone
tabique septum

tálamo thalamus
tallo cerebral brainstem **talón** heel
tejido fibroso fibrous tissue
tejidos tissues
tendón de la corva hamstring
tetilla nipple (male)
tibia shin
timo thymus
tiroides thyroid
trasero buttocks
trompa tube
tronco thorax
tubo digestivo superior upper GI
vejiga bladder
ventanilla nostril
vesícula biliar gallbladder
vías pulmiratorias/ aéreas airways
vientre stomach

CARDIOLOGY

acute infarct scintigraphy gammagrama
de infarto agudo
atrial flutter aleteo auricular
atrial septal defect ASD comunicación
interauricular CIA
balloon (angioplasty) sonda balón
beat later
blood pressure presión arterial
blood pressure presión sanguínea
branches ramas
bundle haz de his
bypass anastomosis quirúrgica
bypass derivación vascular
cardiac arrest paro cardíaco
cardiac output gasto cardíaco
congenital heart defect cardiopatía
congénita
congestive heart failutre insuficiencia
cardiaca congestiva
coronary artery disease arteriopatía
coronaria
coronary heart disease cardiopatía
coronaria
embolism embolio
exhaustion agotamiento
hardening of the arteries endurecimiento
de las arterias
HDL LAD
heart attack infarto de miocardio
heart murmur soplo del corazón
heart rate frecuencia cardiaca
heartbeat latido del corazón
heartburn acidez
IDL LMD
LDL LBD
mediastinal widening linfodenopatía
mediastinal
mesh malla
miocardial infarction infarto del
miocardio
narrowed estrechadas
pacemaker marcapasos
resting pulse pulso en reposo
resuscitation reanimación
ruido bruit
SCD muerte cardiaca repentina
standby pacemaker marcapasos de
demanda
stress test prueba de esfuerzo
thinner diluyente
varicose veins várices

varicose veins venas varicosas
ventrical septal defect comunicación
interventricular

CARDIOLOGÍA

acidez heartburn
agotamiento exhaustion
aleteo auricular atrial flutter
anastomosis quirúrgica bypass
arteriopatía coronaria coronary artery
  disease
bruit ruido
cardiopatía congénita congenital heart
  defect
cardiopatía coronaria coronary heart
  disease
comunicación interauricular CIA atrial
  septal defect ASD
comunicación interventricular ventrical
  septal defect
derivación vascular bypass
diluyente thinner
embolio embolism
endurecimiento de las arterias hardening
  of the arteries
estrechadas narrowed
frecuencia cardiaca heart rate
gammagrama de infarto agudo acute
  infarct scintigraphy
gasto cardiaco cardiac output
haz de his bundle
infarto de miocardio heart attack
infarto del miocardio miocardial
  infarction
insuficiencia cardiaca congestiva
  congestive heart failutre
LAD HDL
later beat
latido del corazón heartbeat
LBD LDL
linfodenopatía mediastinal mediastinal
  widening
LMD IDL
malla mesh
marcapasos pacemaker
marcapasos de demanda standby
  pacemaker
muerte cardiaca repentina SCD
paro cardíaco cardiac arrest
presión arterial blood pressure
presión sanguínea blood pressure
prueba de esfuerzo stress test
pulso en reposo resting pulse
ramas branches
reanimación resuscitation

sonda balón balloon (angioplasty)
soplo del corazón heart murmur **várices**
varicose veins
venas varicosas varicose veins

CLINICAL

attending (physician) adscrito
bandage envoltura
bandage faja
bed rest reposo
bedpan bacinilla
bedpan orinal
bedridden postrado en cama
bland diet régimen de comida no picante
blood culture hemocultivo
blood presssure cuff tensiómetro
blood presssure cuff tensiómetro
blood pressure presión arterial
blood pressure presión sanguínea
blood pressure cuff esfigmomanómetro
blood pressure cuff esfigmomanómetro
boil, abcess absceso
booster shot revacunación
booster shot vacuna de refuerzo
CAT scan tomografía axial computarizada
catheter sonda
catheter tubo de drenado
chart expediente
chart expediente
clamp pinza
compress parche
condition afección
count recuento
crushing (pain) aplastante
CT scan tomografía computarizada
cutterage legrado
discharge escurrimiento
discharge/ to release from the clinic
  dar de alta
DNR órden de no resuscitar
dosage dosificación
dosage posología
dressing vendaje
ear scope otoscopio
early detection detección temprana
enema laxativa
ethnic group pertenencia étnica
followup control
followup seguimiento
fully aware plena conciencia
gash tajo
gauze gasa
guardian tutor legal
gunshot balazo
healthcare proxy poder médico
heating pad cojín eléctrico
heating pad almohadilla eléctrica

height gauge talla
high fiber diet régimen de mucho residuo
history antecedentes
hold aguantar
homeopathic doctor chochero
hospice centro de cuidados paliativos
injection, sting piquete
injured lesionado
jejunum yeyuno
last rites santos óleos
Medicaid Asistencia Médica del gobierno
midwife partera
morgue anfiteatro
morgue depósito de cadáveres
MRI imágenes de resonancia magnética
MRI resonancia magnética nuclear
needle aguja
nerve injury lesiones nerviosas
noxious nocivo
numb adormecido
nurse practititioner enfermero de pratica
  avanzada
nursing home ancianato
office procedure procedimiento en el
  consultório
operating room quirófano
operating table mesa quirúrgica
outpatient, clinic ambulatorio
PCP médico de cabecera
physician's assistant asociado medico
platelet plaqueta
policy póliza
pre-op pre-quirúrgica
prick pinchazo
prick pinchazo
probe probeta
pulmonologist neumólogo
pump bomba
puncture punzada
resident médico en capacitación
scale báscula
scale balanza
scalpel bisturí
scan imagen diagnóstica
screen examen de detección
screening detección sistemática
serum suero
speculum espéculo
stab wound cuchillada
staple grapa
stethescope estetoscopio

stirrup   estribo
stitches   suturas
stitches   puntos
stress   esfuerzo
stress test   prueba de esfuerzo
stretcher   camilla
surgeon   cirujano(a)
surgical needle   aguja para suturas
swab   hisopo
symptom   seña
syringe   jeringa
to bend   agacharse
to bite down   apretar los dientes
to fast (food)   ayunar
to heal   sanar
to kneel   hincarse de rodilla
to lean   inclinarse
to prick   pinchar
to prick   pinchar
to raise   alzar
to spread   propagarse
tongue depressor   abate lengua
tweezers   pinzas
venipuncture   venopunción
work release   relevo de trabajo

CLÍNICO

abate lengua   tongue depressor
absceso   boil, abcess
adormecido   numb
adscrito   attending (physician)
afección   condition
agacharse   to bend
aguantar   hold
aguja   needle
aguja para suturas   surgical needle
almohadilla eléctrica   heating pad
alzar   to raise
ambulatorio   outpatient, clinic
ancianato   nursing home
anfiteatro   morgue
antecedentes   history
aplastante   crushing (pain)
apretar los dientes   to bite down
Asistencia Médica del gobierno
   Medicaid
asociado medico   physician's assistant
ayunar   to fast (food)
bacinilla   bedpan
balanza   scale
balazo   gunshot
báscula   scale
bisturí   scalpel
bomba   pump
camilla   stretcher
centro de cuidados paliativos   hospice
chochero   homeopathic doctor
cirujano(a)   surgeon
cojín eléctrico   heating pad
control   followup
cuchillada   stab wound
dar de alta   discharge/ to release from the
   clinic
depósito de cadáveres   morgue
detección sistemática   screening
detección temprana   early detection
dosificación   dosage
enfermero de pratica avanzada   nurse
   practititioner
envoltura   bandage
escurrimiento   discharge
esfigmomanómetro   blood pressure cuff
esfigmomanómetro   blood pressure cuff
esfuerzo   stress
espéculo   speculum
estetoscopio   stethescope

estribo   stirrup
examen de detección   screen
expediente   chart
expediente   chart
faja   bandage
gasa   gauze
grapa   staple
hemocultivo   blood culture
hincarse de rodilla   to kneel
hisopo   swab
imagen diagnóstica   scan
imágenes de resonancia magnética   MRI
inclinarse   to lean
jeringa   syringe
laxativa   enema
legrado   cutterage
lesionado   injured
lesiones nerviosas   nerve injury
médico de cabecera   PCP
médico em capacitación   resident
mesa quirúrgica   operating table
neumólogo   pulmonologist
nocivo   noxious
órden de no resuscitar   DNR
orinal   bedpan
otoscopio   ear scope
parche   compress
partera   midwife
pertenencia étnica   ethnic group
pinchar   to prick
pinchar   to prick
pinchazo   prick
pinchazo   prick
pinza   clamp
pinzas   tweezers
piquete   injection, sting
plaqueta   platelet
plena conciencia   fully aware
poder médico   healthcare proxy
póliza   policy
posología   dosage
postrado em cama   bedridden
pre-quirúrgica   pre-op
presión arterial   blood pressure
presión sanguínea   blood pressure
probeta   probe
procedimiento em el consultório   office
   procedure
propagarse   to spread
prueba de esfuerzo   stress test

puntos stitches
punzada puncture
quirófano operating room
recuento count **régimen de comida no picante** bland diet
régimen de mucho residuo high fiber diet
relevo de trabajo work release
reposo bed rest
resonancia magnética nuclear MRI
revacunación booster shot
sanar to heal
santos óleos last rites
seguimento followup
seña symptom
sonda catheter
suero serum
suturas stitches
tajo gash
talla height gauge
tensiómetro blood presssure cuff
tensiómetro blood presssure cuff
tomografía axial computarizada CAT scan
tomografía computarizada CT scan
tubo de drenado catheter
tutor legal guardian
vacuna de refuerzo booster shot
vendaje dressing
venopunción venipuncture
yeyuno jejunum

DENTISTRY

bite down (to)   apretar los dientes
bleeding gums   sangrado de encías
buck teeth   dientes salidos
cavity   diente podrido
dental braces   frenos dentales
dental floss   seda dental
denture   dentadura postiza
dentures   caja de dientes
dentures   prótesis dental
fill   obturar
fill   surtir
filling   empaste
floss   hilo dental
grate (to)   rechinar
grinding   rozamiento
gums   encías
incisor   colmillo
molar   muela
noxious   nocivo
orthodontic work   ortodoncia
rinse (to)   enjuagar
root canal   canal en la raíz
root canal   conducto radicular
root canal   tratamiento de conductos
socket   cavidad
tartar   sarro
temporal mandibular joint (TMJ)
   articulación temporomandibular
tooth decay   caries dental
toothache   dolor de muela

ODONTOLOGÍA

apretar los dientes to bite down
articulación temporomandibular
  temporal mandibular joint (TMJ)
caja de dientes dentures
canal en la raíz root canal
caries dental tooth decay
cavidad socket
colmillo incisor
conducto radicular root canal
dentadura postiza denture
diente podrido cavity
dientes salidos buck teeth
dolor de muela toothache
empaste filling
encias gums
enjuagar to rinse
frenos dentales dental braces
hilo dental floss
muela molar
nocivo noxious
obturar fill
ortodoncia orthodontic work
prótesis dental dentures
rechinar to grate
rozamiento grinding
sangrado de encías bleeding gums
sarro tartar
seda dental dental floss
surtir fill
tratamiento de conductos root canal

DERMATOLOGY

abrasion raspadura
abscess hinchazón
adipose tissue grasa subcutánea
athlete's foot hongos en los pies
athlete's foot pie de atleta
athlete's foot tiña podal
baldness alopecia
bedbug chinche
bite mordedura
bite picadura
blister llaga
blister ampolla
body hair vello
boil furúnculo
boil, abcess absceso
bump, cyst, lump bolita
bunion juanete
callus callo
chapped agrietado
cold sore úlcera en los labios
complexion tez
cracked partido
cradle cap costra láctea
cyst quiste
dander caspa
dandruff caspa
dimple hoyuelo
fever blisters llagas de fiebre
flake escama
freckles pecas
frostbite congelación
genital warts condilomas
genital warts verrugas genitales
graft injerto
hangnail padrastro
hangnail uñero
hickey chupón
hive roncha
hives or rash urticaria
ingrown nail uña enterrada
ingrown nail uñero
itch picazón
itching rascazón
jock itch tiña inguinal
lice piojo
lunate semilunar
mole lunar
nit liendre
ointment pomada
ointment ungüento
peeling of the skin descamación de la piel

pimple espinilla
pimple grano
poison oak roble venenoso
pubic hair vello púbico
pubic lice piojo del pubis
pubic lice, crab louse ladilla
radiolunar radiocubital
rash erupción cutánea
rash sarpullido
rash and swelling pasmo
scab costra
scabies escabiosis
scabies sarna
scalp cuero cabelludo
scar cicatriz
scar tissue tejido cicatrizal
skin cutis
sunscreen pantalla solar
tick garrapata
to burn arder
wart verruga
yeast infection hongos vaginales

DERMATOLOGÍA

absceso boil, abcess
agrietado chapped
alopecia baldness
ampolla blister
arder to burn
bolita bump, cyst, lump
callo callus
caspa dander
caspa dandruff
chinche bedbug
chupón hickey
cicatriz scar
condilomas genital warts
congelación frostbite
costra scab
costra láctea cradle cap
cuero cabelludo scalp
cutis skin
descamación de la piel peeling of the skin
erupción cutánea rash
escabiosis scabies
escama flake
espinilla pimple
furúnculo boil
garrapata tick
grano pimple
grasa subcutánea adipose tissue
hinchazón abscess
hongos en los pies athlete's foot
hongos vaginales yeast infection
hoyuelo dimple
injerto graft
juanete bunion
ladilla pubic lice, crab louse
liendre nit
llaga blister
llagas de fiebre fever blisters
lunar mole
mordedura bite
padrastro hangnail
pantalla solar sunscreen
partido cracked
pasmo rash and swelling
pecas freckles
picadura bite
picazón itch
pie de atleta athlete's foot
piojo lice
piojo del pubis pubic lice

pomada ointment
quiste cyst **radiocubital** radiolunar
rascazón itching
raspadura abrasion
roble venenoso poison oak
roncha hive
sarna scabies
sarpullido rash
semilunar lunate
tejido cicatrizal scar tissue
tez complexion
tiña inguinal jock itch
tiña podal athlete's foot
úlcera em los labios cold sore
uña enterrada ingrown nail
uñero hangnail
uñero ingrown nail
ungüento ointment
urticaria hives or rash
vello body hair
vello púbico pubic hair
verruga wart
verrugas genitales genital warts

ENT – EAR, NOSE, AND THROAT
Otolaryngology

Adam's apple nuez de Adán
cleft palate abertura de paladar
cleft palate paladar hendido
croup garrotillo
deaf sordo
dull sordo
ear plugs tapones de oídos
ear scope otoscopio
eardrum tímpano
earwax cera del oído
esophagus boca del estómago
hard of hearing medio sordo
hearing-aid audífono
hoarseness ronco
hoarseness ronquera
nasal cavity hoyo de la nariz
nasal spray atomizador nasal
nostril fosa nasal
otolaryngology otorrinolaringología
palate paladar
pharyngitis faringitis
pharynx faringe
ringing in ears zumbido en los oídos
roof of mouth paladar
sense of smell sentido de olfato
septum tabique
taste (sense) gusto
taste buds papilas gustativas
thorax tronco
to choke atragantarse
to drool babear
tongue depressor abate lengua
tongue depressor bajalenguas
windpipe gaznate

OTORRINOLARINGOLOGÍA

abate lengua tongue depressor
abertura de paladar cleft palate
atomizador nasal nasal spray
atragantarse to choke
audífono hearing-aid
babear to drool
bajalenguas tongue depressor
boca del estómago esophagus
cera del oído earwax
faringe pharynx
faringitis pharyngitis
fosa nasal nostril
garrotillo croup
gaznate windpipe
gusto taste (sense)
hoyo de la nariz nasal cavity
medio sordo hard of hearing
nuez de Adán Adam's apple
otorrinolaringología otolaryngology
otoscopio ear scope
paladar roof of mouth
paladar palate
paladar hendido cleft palate
papilas gustativas taste buds
ronco hoarseness
ronquera hoarseness
sentido de olfato sense of smell
sordo deaf
sordo dull
tabique septum
tapones de oídos ear plugs
tímpano eardrum
tronco thorax
zumbido en los oídos ringing in ears

GASTROENTEROLOGY AND UROLOGY

anus ano
belch eructo
belch regueldo
bile bilis
bile hiel
bloating hinchazón
bloody stool defecación sanguinolenta
bowel movement defecación
chyme quimo
cloudy urine orina turbia
constipated atrancado(a)
constipation estreñimiento
cramps calambres
diarrhea chorrillo
digestive tract tubo digestivo
duodenum duodeno
foreskin prepucio
gallstone cálculo biliar
gallstones piedras biliares
guts tripas
heartburn agruras
heartburn pirosis
hemorrhoids almorranas
hemorrhoids hemorroides
hernia rotura
hookworm anquilostoma
hookworm lombriz de gancho
hookworm nematodo del intestino
indigestion empacho
indigestion entripado
intravenous pyelogram (IVP) urograma
  excretorio
kidney stone cálculo renal
large intestine intestino grueso
laxative laxante
liver hígado
liver failure (severe) insuficiencia hepática
  grave
locked intestine tripa ida
perineum periné
perineum perineo
pinworm gusano pequeño
rectal exam tacto rectal
rectum recto
ringworm tiña
small intestine intestino delgado
sphincter esfinter
squeeze estrujar
stomach vientre
stomach cramp retorcijón
stomach gas pedos

stone cálculo
stool culture coprocultivo
tapeworm solitaria
tapeworm tenia
threadworm oxiuros
tinea tiña
ureter caño de la orina
urethroscope fibroscopio urinario
upper GI tubo digestivo superior
vas deferens conducto deferente

GASTROENTEROLOGÍA Y UROLOGÍA

almorranas hemorrhoids
ano anus
anquilostoma hookworm
atrancado(a) constipated
bilis bile
calambres cramps
cálculo stone
cálculo biliar gallstone
cálculo renal kidney stone
caño de la orina ureter
conducto deferente vas deferens
chorrillo diarrhea
coprocultivo stool culture
defecación bowel movement
defecación sanguinolenta bloody stool
duodeno duodenum
empacho indigestion
entripado indigestion
eructo belch
esfinter sphincter
estreñimiento constipation
estrujar squeeze
fibroscopio urinario urethroscope
gusano pequeño pinworm
hiel bile
hígado liver
hinchazón bloating
insuficiencia hepática grave severe liver
   failure
intestino delgado small intestine
intestino grueso large intestine
laxante laxative
lombriz de gancho hookworm
nematodo del intestino hookworm
orina turbia cloudy urine
oxiuros threadworm
pedos stomach gas
periné perineum
perineo perineum
piedras biliares gallstones
pirosis heartburn
prepucio foreskin
quimo chyme
recto rectum
regueldo belch
repetir to burp
retorcijón stomach cramp
rotura hernia
solitaria tapeworm

tacto rectal rectal exam
tenia tapeworm tiña ringworm
tripa ida locked intestine
tripas guts
tubo digestivo digestive tract
tubo digestivo superior upper GI
urograma excretorio intravenous
pyelogram (IVP)
vejiga bladder
vientre stomach, womb

INFECTIOUS DISEASE AND IMMUNOLOGY

AIDS SIDA
Antibodies anticuerpos
antimalarial antipalúdico
chickenpox varicela
chickenpox viruela loca
congestion catarro
croup garrotillo
flu gripe
gonorrhea purgación
hay fever fiebre de heno
HIV VIH
HIV antibody test prueba de detección
  del VIH
influenza gripe
leprosy lepra
malaria malaria
malaria plaudismo
measles sarampión
mite ácaro
mumps paperas
mumps parótidas
pertussis tos ferina
plague peste
rebound rebote
relapse recaída
rubella rubeola
shingles culebrilla
shingles herpes zoster
sinus seno
smallpox viruela
tetanus tétano
tetanus (shot) antitetánica
thymus timo
to flare up agravarse
triggers provocadores
viral viral
whooping cough tos ferina

ENFERMEDADES INFECCIOSAS Y IMUNOLOGÍA

acaro mite
ADN DNA
agravarse to flare up
anticuerpo antibody
antipalúdico antimalarial
antitetánica tetanus (shot)
catarro congestion
culebrilla singles
fiebre del heno hay fever
garrotillo croup
gripe flu, influenza
herpes zoster shingles
lepra leprosy
malaria malaria
paperas mumps
parótidas mumps
peste plague
plaudismo malaria
prueba de detección del VIH HIV
  antibody test
provocadores triggers
purgación gonorrhea
rebote rebound
recaída relapse
rubeola rubella
sarampion measles
seno sinus
SIDA AIDS
tétano tetanus
timo thymus
tisis tuberculosis (TB)
tos ferina pertussis
tos ferina whooping cough
varicela chickenpox
VIH HIV
viral viral
viruela smallpox
viruela loca chickenpox

LABORATORY AND HEMATOLOGY

blast cell   hemoblasto
blood clot   coágulo de sangre
blood count   biometría hemática
blood culture   hemocultivo
blood type   grupo sanguíneo
blood type   grupo sanguíneo
bloodstream   corriente sanguínea
clotting   coagulación
DNA   ADN
erythrocyte   glóbulo rojo
HDL   LAD
IDL   LMD
LDL   LBD
red blood cell   eritrocito
red blood cell   glóbulo rojo
screen   examen de detección
sed rate (erythrocyte sedimentation rate)
   velocidade de sedimentación globular
sickle cell anemia   anemia de glóbulos
   falciformes
smear   frotis
spleen   bazo
stool culture   coprocultivo
swab   hisopo
vein stripping   extracción de várices
white blood cell   glóbulo blanco
white blood cell   leucocito

LABORATORIO Y HEMATOLOGÍA

ADN DNA
anemia de glóbulos falciformes sickle
  cell anemia
bazo spleen
biometría hemática blood count
coagulación clotting
coágulo de sangre blood clot
coprocultivo stool culture
corriente sanguínea bloodstream
eritrocito red blood cell
examen de detección screen
extracción de várices vein stripping
frotis smear
glóbulo blanco white blood cell
glóbulo rojo erythrocyte
glóbulo rojo red blood cell
grupo sanguíneo blood type
grupo sanguíneo blood type
hemoblasto blast cell
hemocultivo blood culture
hisopo swab
LAD HDL
LBD LDL
leucocito white blood cell
LMD IDL
velocidade de sedimentación globular
  sed rate (erythrocyte sedimentation rate)

NEPHROLOGY AND ENDICRINOLOGY

adrenal gland glándula suprarrenal
goiter bocio
insulin pen lapicero de insulina
jet injector inyector a chorro
ketone cetona
kidney riñón
kidney failure insuficiencia renal
kidney stones piedras renales
renal failure insuficiencia renal
strips tiras
thyroid tiroides

NEFROLOGÍA Y ENDOCRINOLOGÍA

bocio goiter
cetona ketone
glándula suprarrenal adrenal gland
infusor infuser
insuficiencia renal kidney failure, renal
  failure
inyector a chorro jet injector
lapicero de insulina insulin pen
piedras renales kidney stones
riñón kidney
tiras strips
tiroides thyroid

NEUROLOGY

blackouts desmayos
brain fissure cisura cerebral
brain scan imagen del cerebro
brain, cerebrum cerebro
brains sesos
brainstem tallo cerebral
cerebellum cerebelo
medulla tuétano
myoclonic seizure mioclonía
nuclear brain scan gammagrama cerebral
skull cráneo
spinal cord médula espinal
spinal tap drenaje espinal
spinal tap punción lumbar
stroke apoplejía
stroke derrame cerebral
stroke embolia
tangles marañas

NEUROLOOGÍA

apoplejía stroke
cerebelo cerebellum
cerebro brain, cerebrum
cisura cerebral brain fissure
cráneo skull
derrame cerebral stroke
desmayos blackouts
drenaje espinal spinal tap
embolia stroke
escape aórtico aortic leakage
gammagrama cerebral nuclear brain scan
imagen del cerebro brain scan
marañas tangles
médula espinal spinal cord
mioclonía myoclonic seizure
punción lumbar spinal tap
sesos brains
soplo aneurismático aneurismal murmur
tallo cerebral brainstem
tuétano medulla

OBSTETRICS AND GYNECOLOGY

abortion   aborto inducido
abruptio placentae   desprendimiento prematuro de la placenta
Agpar test   escala de Agpar
amniotic fluid   líquido amniótico
bag of waters   fuente
bloody show   desecho con sangre
breast engorgement   atiborramiento de senos
breast feeding, to nurse   amamantar
breast pump   bomba para senos
breast tenderness   mastalgia
breech   de nalgas
cervical cap   capuchón cervical
cervix   cuello del útero
condom   preservativo
contraceptive   anticonceptivo
cravings   antojos
crowning   aparición de la cabeza fetal
curettage   curetaje
curettage   raspado
cutterage   legrado
D&C   dilatación y raspado
delivery   expulsión del feto
delivery, labor, childbirth   parto
discharge   escurrimiento
douche   lavada
due date   fecha estimada de parto
effacement of the cervix   borramiento del cuello
embryo   embrión
estrogen   estrógeno
estrogen replacement therapy   terapia sustitutiva de estrógenos
expectant mother   gestante
fallopian tube   trompa de Falopio
false labor   parto falso
fertilization, fecundation   fecundación
fetal distress   sufrimiento fetal
fetal monitoring   cardiotecografía
fetus   feto
fibroid   fibromioma
fibroid   mioma
gonorrhea   purgación
hot flashes   bochornos
hot flashes   calores
hot flashes   sofoco
intrauterine device   dispositivo intrauterino
IUD   DIU
labor (final)   alumbramiento

lacerated cervix   cuello desgarrado
letdown   reflejo del chorro de leche
lochia   loquios
lump   bulto
midwife   matrona
midwife   partera
miscarriage   aborto espontáneo
morning sickness   malestar matutino
mucous plug   tapón mucoso
nipple (female)   pezón
ovarian cyst   quiste ovárico
pap smear   citología vaginal
pap smear   prueba de Papanicolau
Pap test   examen de Papanicolaou
period, menstruation   regla
polyp   pólipo
prelabor   antes del parto
prolapse of the uterus   caída de la matriz
quadruplet   cuatrillizo
quintuplet   quintillizo
sanitary pads   toallas
sitz bath   baño de asiento
sonogram, ultrasound   ecografía
spotting   manchas de flujo vaginal con sangre
spotting   sangrado ligero
stillbirth   nacimiento de bebé muerto
stillborn   nacido muerto
stirrup   estribo
stretch mark   estría
suction   succión
suction curettage   aspiración con vacío
suppository   óvulo
sweats   sudores
to deliver, give birth   dar a luz
triplet   trillizo
tubal ligation   ligadura de trompas/ tubos
tubal pregnancy   embarazo tubárico
tube   trompa
twin (fraternal)   cuate
twin (fraternal)   mellizo
twin (identical)   gemelo
varicose veins   várices
varicose veins   venas varicosas
womb   matriz
yeast   hongos
yeast infection   micosis vaginal

OBSTETRICIA Y GINECOLOGÍA

aborto espontáneo miscarriage
aborto inducido abortion
alumbramiento labor (final)
amamantar breast feeding, to nurse
antes del parto prelabor
anticonceptivo contraceptive
antojos cravings
aparición de la cabeza fetal crowning
aspiración con vacío suction curettage
atiborramiento de senos breast
  engorgement
baño de asiento sitz bath
bochornos hot flashes
bomba para senos breast pump
borramiento del cuello effacement of the
  cervix
bulto lump
caída de la matriz prolapse of the uterus
calores hot flashes
capuchón cervical cervical cap
cardiotecografía fetal monitoring
citología vaginal pap smear
cuate twin (fraternal)
cuatrillizo quadruplet
cuello del útero cervix
cuello desgarrado lacerated cervix
curetaje curettage
dar a luz to deliver, give birth
de nalgas breech
desecho con sangre bloody show
**desprendimiento prematuro de la
placenta** abruptio placentae
dilatación y raspado D&C
dispositivo intrauterino intrauterine
  device
DIU IUD
ecografía sonogram, ultrasound
embarazo tubárico tubal pregnancy
embrión embryo
escala de Agpar Agpar test
escurrimiento discharge
estría stretch mark
estribo stirrup
estrógeno estrogen
examen de Papanicolaou Pap test
expulsión del feto delivery
fecha estimada de parto due date
fecundación fertilization, fecundation
feto fetus
fibromioma fibroid

fuente bag of waters
gemelo twin (identical)
gestante expectant mother
hongos yeast
lavada douche
legrado cutterage
ligadura de trompas/ tubos tubal
  ligation
líquido amniótico amniotic fluid
loquios lochia
malestar matutino morning sickness
manchas de flujo vaginal con sangre
  spotting
mastalgia breast tenderness
matriz womb
matrona midwife
mellizo twin (fraternal)
micosis vaginal yeast infection
mioma fibroid
nacido muerto stillborn
nacimiento de bebé muerto stillbirth
óvulo suppository
partera midwife
parto delivery, labor, childbirth
parto falso false labor
pezón nipple (female)
pólipo polyp
preservativo condom
prueba de Papanicolau pap smear
purgación gonorrhea
quintillizo quintuplet
quiste ovárico ovarian cyst
raspado curettage
reflejo del chorro de leche letdown
regla period, menstruation
sangrado ligero spotting
sofoco hot flashes
succión suction
sudores sweats
sufrimiento fetal fetal distress
tapón mucoso mucous plug
terapéutica substitutiva de estrógenos
  estrogen replacement therapy
toallas sanitary pads
trillizo triplet
trompa tube
trompa de Falopio fallopian tube
várices varicose veins
venas varicosas varicose veins

ONCOLOGY

adrenal cancer cáncer de las glándulas
suprarenales
cáncer en cuirasse cáncer progresivo del
tórax
clinical trial ensayo clínico
leukemia leucemia
lump bulto
lymph linfa
lymph node ganglio linfático
lymphocyte linfocito
tumor incordio

ONCOLOGÍA

bulto lump
cáncer de las glándulas suprarenales
   adrenal cancer
cáncer progresivo del tórax   cáncer en
   cuirasse
ensayo clínico   clinical trial
ganglio linfático   lymph node
incordio   tumor
leucemia   leukemia
linfa   lymph
linfocito   lymphocyte
médula ósea   bone marrow

OPHTHALMOLOGY

blinking parpadeo
blurred vision vista nublada
color blind daltónico
contact lenses pupilentes
corner of the eye ángulo del ojo
cross-eyed bizco
cross-eyed turnio
dark circles under eyes ojeras
detached retina desprendimiento de
  retina
eye scope oftalmoscopio
eyeball globo del ojo
eyedropper cuentagotas
eyelid párpado
farsighted hipermétrope
nearsighted miope
sclera esclerótica
socket cuenca
strabismus, cross-eye estrabismo
sty orzuelo
tear duct conduto lacrimal
to squint fruncir
to squint mirar entecerrado
vision chart cuadro de agudeza visual

OFTALMOLOGÍA

ángulo del ojo   corner of the eye
bizco   cross-eyed
conduto lacrimal   tear duct
cuadro de agudeza visual   vision chart
cuenca   socket
cuentagotas   eyedropper
daltónico   color blind
desprendimiento de retina   detached
   retina
esclerótica   sclera
estrabismo   strabismus, cross-eye
fruncir   to squint
globo del ojo   eyeball
hipermétrope   farsighted
miope   nearsighted
mirar entecerrado   to squint
oftalmoscopio   eye scope
ojeras   dark circles under eyes
orzuelo   sty
parpadeo   blinking
párpado   eyelid
pupilentes   contact lenses
turnio   cross-eyed
vista nublada   blurred vision

ORTHOPEDICS

ankle tobillo
arch support sostén del arco
back brace braguero
back brace espaldera
backbone espinazo
ball and socket joint cabeza y cavidad
  articular
belt faja
bone infarction infarto óseo
bone marrow médula ósea
bow-legged chueco
bow-legged zambo
brace aparato ortopédico
cane bastón
carpal carpiana
carpal tunnel syndrome síndrome de
  túnel carpiano
cast yeso
charley horse agujeta
clubfoot pie torcido
compound fracture fractura abierta
crack trueno
crick in neck tortícolis
crippled tullido
crutches muletas
dislocated zafado
dislocation descoyuntura
dislocation desencaje
dislocation recalcada
dislocation zafadura
elbow codo
fibula peroné
flatfoot pie plano
fontanel mollera
fracture quebradura
hairline fracture fisura
hamstring tendón de la corva
in a cast enyesado
instep empeine
joint articulación
joint cavity cavidad articular
kneecap rótula
limp renguear
lock-jaw trismo
nape nuca
orthopedic brace férula para miembros
osteoarthritis artrosis
osteogenic sarcoma osteosarcoma
patellofemoral femororrotuliana
physical therapy fisioterapia
popping crujido

puffiness inflamación
pulled muscle tirón
radiocarpal radiocarpiana
rib costilla
rib cage caja torácica
rickets raquitismo
rotator cuff rotador del hombro
ruptured disk disco roto
sling cabestrillo
sling honda
slipped disk disco desplazado
slipped disk disco zafado
spinal column columna vertebral
spine espina dorsal
spine espina vertebral
splint férula
splint tablilla
sprain esguince
sprain falseado
sprain torcedura
spur espolón
spur esquince
sternum esternón
stiff tieso
stiff neck cuello rígido
straight cane bordón
subtalar subastragalina
tailbone cóccix
tailbone colita
talofibular ligament ligamento
  peroneoastragalino
talus astrágalo
tear desgarre
tear a ligament desgarrar um ligamento
temporal mandibular joint (TMJ)
  articulación temporomandibular
to crack tronar
to lock up atorar
torn ligament desgarramiento
torn ligament esguince
whiplash desnucamiento
wrist muñeca

ORTOPEDIA

agujeta   charley horse
aparato ortopédico   brace
articulación   joint
articulación temporomandibular
   temporal mandibular joint (TMJ)
artrosis   osteoarthritis
astrágalo   talus
atorar   to lock up
bastón   cane
bordón   straight cane
braguero   back brace
cabestrillo   sling
cabeza y cavidad articular   ball and
   socket joint
caja torácica   rib cage
carpiana   carpal
cavidad articular   joint cavity
chueco   bow-legged
cóccix   tailbone
codo   elbow
colita   tailbone
columna vertebral   spinal column
costilla   rib
crujido   popping
cuello rígido   stiff neck
descoyuntura   dislocation
desencaje   dislocation
desgarramiento   torn ligament
desgarrar um ligamento   tear a ligament
desgarre   tear
desnucamiento   whiplash
disco desplazado   slipped disk
disco roto   ruptured disk
disco zafado   slipped disk
empeine   instep
enyesado   in a cast
esguince   sprain
esguince   torn ligament
espaldera   back brace
espina dorsal   spine
espina vertebral   spine
espinazo   backbone
espolón   spur
esquince   spur
esternón   sternum
faja   belt
falseado   sprain
femororrotuliana   patellofemoral
férula   splint
férula para miembros   orthopedic brace

fisioterapia   physical therapy
fisura   hairline fracture
fractura abierta   compound fracture
honda   sling
infarto óseo   bone infarction
inflamación   puffiness
ligamento peroneoastragalino   talofibular
   ligament
médula ósea   bone marrow
maoller   fontanel
muletas   crutches
muñeca   wrist
nuca   nape
osteosarcoma   osteogenic sarcoma
peroné   fibula
pie plano   flatfoot
pie torcido   clubfoot
quebradura   fracture
radiocarpiana   radiocarpal
raquitismo   rickets
recalcada   dislocation
renguear   limp
rotador del hombro   rotator cuff
rótula   kneecap
síndrome de túnel carpiano   carpal tunnel
   syndrome
sostén del arco   arch support
subastragalina   subtalar
tablilla   splint
tendón de la corva   hamstring
tieso   stiff
tirón   pulled muscle
tobillo   ankle
torcedura   sprain
tortícolis   crick in neck
trismo   lock-jaw
tronar   to crack
trueno   crack
tullido   crippled
yeso   cast
zafado   dislocated
zafadura   dislocation
zambo   bow-legged

PEDIATRICS

booster shot revacunación
booster shot vacuna de refuerzo
bow-legged chueco
bow-legged zambo
breast feeding, to nurse amamantar
cerebral palsy parálisis cerebral
chickenpox varicela
chickenpox viruela loca
cleft lip cucho
cleft lip labio leporino
colic retorcijón
crib cuna
diaper pañal
diaper rash pañalitis
diaper-urine test (PKU) fenilquetonuria
guardian tutor legal
harelip labio leporino
height, stature estatura
jaundice ictericia
lead poisoning intoxicación por plomo
lead poisoning saturnismo
measles sarampión
MMR triple viral
mumps paperas
mumps parótidas
nit liendre
person with Down's syndrome
  mongólico
poisoned intoxicado
puberty pubertad
rubella rubeola
sleepwalking sonambulismo
smallpox vaccine vacuna antivariólica
tetanus tétano
tetanus (shot) antitetánica
to burp repetir
to spit (up) escupir
to wean destetar
tonsillitis amigdalitis
tonsils agallas
tonsils amígdalas
triplet trillizo
twin (fraternal) cuate
vaccine vacuna

PEDIATRÍA

agallas tonsils
amamantar breast feeding, to nurse
amígdalas tonsils
amigdalitis tonsillitis
antitetánica tetanus (shot)
chueco bow-legged
cuate twin (fraternal)
cucho cleft lip
cuna crib
destetar to wean
escupir to spit (up)
estatura height, stature
fenilquetonuria diaper-urine test (PKU)
ictericia jaundice
intoxicación por plomo lead poisoning
intoxicado poisoned
labio leporino cleft lip
labio leporino harelip
liendre nit
mongólico(a) person with Down's
  syndrome
pañal diaper
pañalitis diaper rash
paperas mumps
parálisis cerebral cerebral palsy
parótidas mumps
pubertad puberty
repetir to burp
retorcijón colic
revacunación booster shot
rubeola rubella
sarampion measles
saturnismo lead poisoning
sonambulismo sleepwalking
tétano tetanus
trillizo triplet
triple viral MMR
tutor legal guardian
vacuna vaccine
vacuna antivariólica smallpox vaccine
vacuna de refuerzo booster shot
varicela chickenpox
viruela loca chickenpox
zambo bow-legged

PHARMACY

acetaminophen paracetamol
active ingredient principio activo
albuterol salbutamol
antibodies anticuerpos
antimalarial antipalúdico
antipyretic antifebril
back brace braguero
bandage envoltura
bandage faja
breast pump bomba para senos
by mouth por vía bucal
compress parche
condom preservativo
contact lenses pupilentes
counteract contrarrestar
crush machucar
decongestant descongestivo
dosage dosificación
dosage posología
dose dosis
eyedropper cuentagotas
gargle hacer gárgaras
gauze gasa
hearing-aid audífono
inhaler inhalador
laxative laxante
laxative purgante
nasal spray atomizador nasal
ointment pomada
overdose sobredosis
painkiller analgésico
patch parche
prescription receta médica
safety pins ganchos
sanitary pads toallas
serum suero
shaft mango
side effect reacción adversa
sitz bath baño de asiento
sling cabestrillo
smallpox vaccine vacuna antivariólica
speculum espéculo
stethescope estetoscopio
straight cane bordón
sunscreen pantalla solar
suppository calía
to fast (food) ayunar
vaccine vacuna
ventilator Pulmirador
vertigo vahído
withdrawal privación

withdrawal symptoms síntomas de desintoxicación

FARMACIA

analgésico painkiller
anticuerpos antibodies
antifebril antipyretic
antipalúdico antimalarial
atomizador nasal nasal spray
audífono hearing-aid
ayunar to fast (food)
baño de asiento sitz bath
bomba para senos breast pump
bordón straight cane
braguero back brace
cabestrillo sling
calía suppository
contrarrestar counteract
cuentagotas eyedropper
descongestivo decongestant
dosificación dosage
dosis dose
envoltura bandage
espéculo speculum
estetoscopio stethescope
faja bandage
ganchos safety pins
gasa gauze
hacer gárgaras gargle
inhalador inhaler
laxante laxative
machucar crush
mango shaft
pantalla solar sunscreen
paracetamol acetaminophen
parche compress
parche patch
pomada ointment
por vía bucal by mouth
posología dosage
preservativo condom
principio activo active ingredient
privación withdrawal
Pulmirador ventilator
pupilentes contact lenses
purgante laxative
reacción adversa side effect
receta médica prescription
salbutamol albuterol
síntomas de desintoxicación withdrawal
  symptoms
sobredosis overdose
suero serum
toallas sanitary pads

vacuna vaccine
vacuna antivariólica smallpox vaccine
vahído vertigo

PSYCHOLOGY

absent-minded olvidadizo
anxiety ansiedad
beating paliza
counseling asesoría
counseling consejería
helplessness impotencia
mental clinic manicomio
mood disorder trastorno del estado de
ánimo
nervous breakdown crisis nerviosa
overdose sobredosis
relapse recaída
restlessness desasosiego
sedative, tranquilizer sedante
shelter asilo
shock therapy terapia electroconvulsiva
sober sobrio
surveillance vigilancia
to hang ahorcar
tranquilizer, sedative calmante
withdrawal abstinencia
withdrawal privación
withdrawal symptoms síntomas de
desintoxicación
worthlessness inutilidad

PSICOLOGÍA

abstinencia withdrawal
ahorcar to hang
ansiedad anxiety
asesoría counseling
asilo shelter
calmante tranquilizer, sedative
consejería counseling
crisis nerviosa nervous breakdown
desasosiego restlessness
impotencia helplessness
inutilidad worthlessness
manicomio mental Clinic
olvidadizo absent-minded
paliza beating
privación withdrawal
recaída relapse
sedante sedative, tranquilizer
síntomas de desintoxicación withdrawal
   symptoms
sobredosis overdose
sobrio sober
terapia electroconvulsiva shock therapy
trastorno del estado de ánimo mood
   disorder
vigilancia surveillance

PULMONOLOGY

airways vías pulmiratorias/ aéreas
albuterol salbutamol
barachial braquial
breath respiración
bronchitis catarro al pecho
bronchitis inflamación de los bofes
deep hondo
expire vencer
expire air espirar
hold aguantar
inhaler inhalador
lung pulmón
mucus moco
nostril ventanilla
pulmonologist neumólogo
shortness of breath ahogo
shortness of breath disnea
shortness of breath sensación de ahogo
sphygmomanometer baumanómetro
spirometer espirómetro
sputum esputo
to pant jadear
ventilator pulmirador
walking pneumonia neumonía migratoria
wheeze chillarle el pecho
wheeze silbido
wheezing sibilancias
wheezing Pulmiración sibilante/ silbante
whistling chiflido

NEUMOLOGÍA

aguantar hold
ahogo shortness of breath
baumanómetro sphygmomanometer
braquial barachial
catarro al pecho bronchitis
chiflido whistling
chillarle el pecho wheeze
disnea shortness of breath
espirar expire air
espirómetro spirometer
esputo sputum
hondo deep
infamación de los bofes bronchitis
inhalador inhaler
jadear to pant
moco mucus
neumólogo pulmonologist
neumonía migratoria walking pneumonia
pulmiración sibilante/ silbante
   wheezing
pulmirador ventilator
pulmón lung
respiración breath
salbutamol albuterol
sensación de ahogo shortness of breath
sibilancias wheezing
silbido wheeze
vencer expire
ventanilla nostril
vías Pulmiratorias/ aéreas airways

SYMPTOMS

abrasion raspadura
abscess postema
abscess tacotillo
acute agudo
anxiety ansiedad
bad breath mal aliento
baldness alopecia
belch eructo
belch regueldo
bleeding gums sangrado de encías
blister llaga
blister ampolla
bloating hinchazón
blood clot coágulo de sangre
bloody stool defecación sanguinolenta
bruise morado
bruise morete
bruise moretón
bulge prominencia
bump topetazo
bump (head) chichón
bump, lump abultamiento
burn (to) arder
burning sensation quemazón
chapped agrietado
chapped lips labios resecos
charley horse agujeta
chills escalofríos
chills temblorina
choke (to) atragantarse
cloudy urine orina turbia
cluster headache cefalea en grupos
cold sore úlcera en los labios
coming and going intermitente
congestion catarro
constipated atrancado(a)
constipation estreñimiento
cracked partido
cramps calambres
cravings antojos
crick in neck tortícolis
crushing (pain) aplastante
dandruff caspa
dark circles under eyes ojeras
dazed atarantado
dazed aturdido
descended prolapso
diarrhea chorrillo
discharge derrame
discomfort molestia
dizziness tarantas

drool (to) babear
drowsy soñoliento
dull sordo
engorgement ingurgitación
exhaustion agotamiento
faint (to) desmayarse
fever blister fuego
fever blisters fogazos
fever blisters llagas de fiebre
flake escama
flare up (to) agravarse
flushed sonrojado
flushed, to become ruborizarse
frostbite congelación
grinding rozamiento
hard of hearing medio sordo
hard tumor cirro
headache cefalea
heartburn acidez
heartburn agruras
heartburn pirosis
hematoma moretón
hemorrhoids almorranas
hiccups hipo
hoarseness ronco
hot flashes bochornos
hot flashes calores
indigestion entripado
inflammation hinchazón
limp cojear
lisping ceceo
lock up (to) atorar
lump protuberancia
malnourished desnutrido(a)
migraine jaqueca
moan (to) gemir
mucus moco
numb adormecido
numb entumecido
numbness entumecimiento
pant (to) jadear
phlegm flema
popping crujido
puffiness inflamación
puffiness hinchazón
rash and swelling pasmo
restlessness inquietud
scab costra
scar cicatriz
scratch (to) rasguñar
seizure ataque

shake (to)   agitar
sharp   agudo
shortness of breath   ahogo
shortness of breath   disnea
shortness of breath   sensación de ahogo
sickle cell anemia   anemia de glóbulos
   falciformes
side stitch   ijada
sinus   seno
sliding scale   escala móvil
sore (open)   llaga abierta
speech difficulties   trastornos del habla
spell   ataque de
sneeze (to)   estornudar
snore (to)   roncar
sputum   esputo
spread (to)   propagarse
stabbing   picante
stomach cramp   retorcijón
stomach gas   pedos
stuffy nose   nariz tapada
stuttering   tartamudeo
sudden   súbito
swelling   hinchazón
swollen, bloated   hinchado
symptom   padecimiento
systemic weakness   achaque
threshhold   umbral
throb (to)   palpitar
throbbing   punzante
tight chest   tensión en el pecho
tingle   hormiguear
twitch (to)   crisparse
twitch   contracción espasmódica
twitch   movimiento espasmódico
twitch   contorsión
twitch   sacudida nerviosa
upset   revuelto
wheeze   chillarle el pecho
wheeze   silbido
wheezing   sibilancias
whistling   chiflido**tumor**   incordio
yawn (to)   bostezar

SÍNTOMAS

abultamiento bump, lump
achaque systemic weakness
acidez heartburn
adormecido numb
agitar to shake
agotamiento exhaustion
agravarse to flare up
agrietado chapped
agruras heartburn
agudo acute
agudo sharp
agujeta charley horse
ahogo shortness of breath
almorranas hemorrhoids
alopecia baldness
ampolla blister
anemia de glóbulos falciformes sickle
  cell anemia
ansiedad anxiety
antojos cravings
aplastante crushing (pain)
arder to burn
ataque seizure
ataque de spell
atarantado dazed
atorar to lock up
atragantarse to choke
atrancado(a) constipated
aturdido dazed
babear to drool
bochornos hot flashes
bostezar to yawn
calambres cramps
calores hot flashes
caspa dandruff
catarro congestion
ceceo lisping
cefalea headache
cefalea en grupos cluster headache
chichón bump (head)
chiflido whistling
chillarle el pecho wheeze
chorrillo diarrhea
cicatriz scar
cirro hard tumor
coágulo de sangre blood clot
cojear limp
congelación frostbite
contorsión twitch
contracción espasmódica twitch
costra scab

crisparse to twitch
crujido popping
defecación sanguinolenta bloody stool
derrame discharge
desmayarse to faint
desnutrido(a) malnourished
disnea shortness of breath
entripado indigestion
entumecido numb
entumecimiento numbness
eructo belch
escala móvil sliding scale
escalofríos chills
escamanu flake
esputo sputum
estornudar to sneeze
estreñimiento constipation
flema phlegm
fogazos fever blisters
fuego fever blister
gemir to moan
hinchado swollen, bloated
hinchazón bloating
hinchazón swelling, inflammation,
  puffiness
hipo hiccups
hormiguear tingle
ijada side stitch
incordio tumor
inflamación puffiness
ingurgitación engorgement
inquietud restlessness
intermitente coming and going
jadear to pant
jaqueca migraine
labios resecos chapped lips
llaga blister
llaga abierta sore (open)
llagas de fiebre fever blisters
mal aliento bad breath
medio sordo hard of hearing
moco mucus
molestia discomfort
morado bruise
morete bruise
moretón bruise
moretón hematoma
movimiento espasmódico twitch
nariz tapada stuffy nose
ojeras dark circles under eyes
orina turbia cloudy urine

padecimiento symptom
palpitar to throb
partido cracked
pasmo rash and swelling
pedos stomach gas
picante stabbing
pirosis heartburn
postema abscess
prolapso descended
prominencia bulge
propagarse to spread
protuberancia lump
punzante throbbing
quemazón burning sensation
rasguñar to scratch
raspadura abrasion
regueldo belch
retorcijón stomach cramp
revuelto upset
roncar to snore
ronco hoarseness
rozamiento grinding
ruborizarse to become flushed
sacudida nerviosa twitch
desecho con sangre bleeding gums
seno sinus
sensación de ahogo shortness of breath
sibilancias wheezing
silbido wheeze
soñoliento drowsy
sonrojado flushed
sordo dull
súbito sudden
tacotillo abscess
tarantas dizziness
tartamudeo stuttering
temblorina chills
tensión en el pecho tight chest
topetazo bump
tortícolis crick in neck
trastornos del habla speech difficulties
úlcera em los labios cold sore
umbral threshhold

4 FALSE COGNATES* IN MEDICINE

These apparent cognate forms have a different meaning in translation

ENGLISH COGNATE		SPANISH MEANING		SPANISH COGNATE		ENGLISH MEANING
anxious	=	agitado	≠	ansioso	=	worried
ability	=	capacidad	≠	habilidad	=	skill
abortion	=	aborto inducido	≠	aborto	=	miscarriage,abortion
abuse	=	maltrato	≠	abusar	=	take advantage
accost	=	abordar	≠	acostar	=	lay down
asylum	=	manicomio	≠	asilo	=	home (senior, etc.)
bigot	=	racista	≠	bigote	=	mustache
choke	=	ahogo	≠	choque	=	shock
cigar	=	puro	≠	cigarro	=	cigarette
colored	=	teñido	≠	colorado	=	red
complexion	=	cutis	≠	complexión	=	disposition
confidence	=	confianza	≠	confidencia	=	secret or private
constipated	=	estreñido	≠	constipado	=	have a cold
control	=	gestionar	≠	control	=	followup
convenience	=	comodidad	≠	conveniencia	=	conformity
courage	=	valor	≠	coraje	=	rage
date	=	fecha	≠	dato	=	data
discharge	=	dar de alta	≠	descargar	=	unload or shoot
dismay	=	desaliento	≠	desmayar	=	to faint
distress	=	angustia	≠	destreza	=	skill
divest	=	renunciar	≠	desvestir	=	undress
druggist	=	farmacéutico	≠	droguista	=	drug dealer
embarrassed	=	avergonzado	≠	embarazada	=	pregnant
examination	=	reconocimiento	≠	examinación	=	test
exit	=	salida	≠	éxito	=	success
expedient	=	ventajoso	≠	expediente	=	file
expedite	=	apresurar	≠	expedir	=	dispatch
finality	=	definitivo	≠	finalidad	=	goal
ignore	=	desconocer	≠	ignorar	=	to be unaware

FALSE COGNATES

ENGLISH COGNATE		SPANISH MEANING		SPANISH COGNATE		ENGLISH MEANING
illiterate	=	analfabeto	≠	iliterato	=	ignorant
inconvienience	=	incomodidad	≠	inconveniencia	=	impropriety
indications	=	pistas	≠	indicaciónes	=	instructions
infant	=	bebé	≠	infant	=	infantryman
infirm	=	enfermizo	≠	enfermo	=	sick
injury	=	herida	≠	injuria	=	insult
intoxicate	=	envenenar	≠	intoxicar	=	poison, to
labor	=	parto	≠	labor	=	work
measure	=	medidap	≠	mesura	=	moderation
miserable	=	triste	≠	miserable	=	destitute
murmur (heart)	=	soplo	≠	murmura	=	gossip
pain	=	dolor	≠	pena	=	pity
parent	=	padre	≠	pariente	=	relative
pathetic	=	lastimoso	≠	patético	=	tragic
peculiar	=	raro	≠	peculiar	=	typical
pinch	=	pellizcar	≠	pinchar	=	puncture
prescription	=	receta	≠	prescripción	=	mandate
pretend	=	finger	≠	pretender	=	purport
prevent	=	impeder	≠	prevenir	=	to warn
probe	=	sonda	≠	prueba	=	test, sample
probe, to	=	sondear	≠	probar	=	to prove, try
quiet	=	callado	≠	quieto	=	tranquil
quit	=	dejar de	≠	quitar	=	take away
rape	=	violar	≠	rapar	=	to shame
relative	=	pariente	≠	relative	=	with respect to
remove	=	quitar	≠	remover	=	to stir
rest	=	descansar	≠	restar	=	subtract
scale	=	balanza	≠	escala	=	measurement scale
temple	=	sien	≠	templo	=	temple (religious)
tutor	=	maestro privado	≠	tutor	=	guardian
vase	=	florero	≠	vaso	=	blood vessel

Note: Only medical and related terminology is considered in this list. Some of these terms are not actually false cognates, but "false friends," as they have similar etymologies, but their modern meanings nevertheless are dissimilar. Definitions are simplified for explanatory purposes; many of these terms yield additional meanings in translation.

5 MORE THAN COGNATES

These medical cognates are valid translations, but they have a potentially
confusing secondary translation

SPANISH COGNATE		ENGLISH COGNATE		ENGLISH MEANING
aborto	=	abortion	=	miscarriage
admitir	=	admit	=	permit
angina	=	angina	=	throat problems
consenter	=	consent	=	pamper, spoil
control	=	control	=	followup, monitor
cuestión	=	question	=	issue, topic
cura	=	cure	=	priest
defraudar	=	defraud	=	disappoint, frustrate
diario	=	diary	=	daily
dignidad	=	dignity	=	rank, post
dispensar	=	dispense	=	grant honors, excuse
ducha	=	douche	=	shower
entero	=	entire	=	full
escuálido	=	squalid	=	skinny
espina	=	spine	=	thorny, difficult
exagerar	=	exaggerate	=	overdo, overstate
extender	=	extend	=	issue, draw up
físico	=	physique	=	physicist
gota	=	gout	=	droplet
inconsciente	=	unconscious	=	irresponsible
incontinente	=	incontinent	=	immediate
lunar	=	lunar	=	mole
manifestación	=	manifestation	=	demonstration
memoria	=	memory	=	report
murmurar	=	murmur	=	gossip
observación	=	observation	=	reprimand
registrar	=	register	=	inspect

Note: Only medical and related terminology is considered in this list.

6 GREEK AND LATIN MEDICAL ROOTS

ENGLISH ROOT	ENGLISH EXAMPLE	SPANISH ROOT	SPANISH EXAMPLE
abdomen	abdominal	abdomen	abdominal
adeno	adenoma	adeno	adenoma
adip	adipose	adip	adipose
bio	biology	bio	biología
carcin	carcinogenic	carcin	carcinógeno
cardi	cardiology	cardi	cardiología
cephal	cephalic	cefal	cefálico
cerebr	cerebral	cerebr	cerebral
cervic	cervical	cervic	cervical
chondr	hypochondria	condr	hipocondríaco
chrom	chromosome	crom	cromosoma
cyst	cystitis	cist	cystitis
cyt	cytology	cit	citología
derm	dermatologist	derm	dermatólogo
dist	distal	dist	distal
dors	dorsal	dors	dorsal
encephal	encephalitis	encefal	encephalitis
enter	gastroenterologist	enter	gastroenterólogo
erythr	erythrocytes	erit	eritrocitos
gastr	gastritis	gastr	gastritis
gnos	diagnosis	gnos	diagnosis
gynec	gynecologist	ginec	ginecólogo
hem	hemorrhoids	hem	hemorroides
hemat	hematoma	hemat	hematoma
hepat	hepatitis	hepat	hepatitis
heter	heterogeneity	heter	heterogeneidad
hist	antihistamine	hist	antihistamínico
hom	homeopathic	hom	homeopático
hydr	hydrate	hidr	hidratar
hyster	hysterectomy	hister	histerectomía
iatr	geriatric	iatr	geriátrico
inguin	sanguine	inguin	sanguíneo
kary	karyokinesis	cari	karyokinesis
lacri	lacrimal	lagrim	lagrimal
lapar	laparoscopic	lapar	laparoscópica
later	lateral	later	lateral
leuk	leukemia	leuc	leukemia
log	logopedics	log	logopedia
lumb	lumbar	lumb	lumbar
medi	mediastanal	medi	mediastanal

GREEK AND LATIN MEDICAL ROOTS

ENGLISH ROOT	ENGLISH EXAMPLE	**SPANISH ROOT**	SPANISH EXAMPLE
mes	mesenchyme	mes	mesénquima
my	myoclonic	mi	mioclónica
myel	myelin	miel	mielina
nas	nasal	nas	nasal
necr	necrosis	necr	necrosis
nephr	nephrology	nefr	nefrología
neur	neurology	neur	neurología
noct	nocturnal	noct	nocturne
omphalo	omphalomesenteric	omfal	onfalomesentérico
onc	oncologist	onc	oncólogo
onych	onycholysis	onic	onicolisis
ophthalm	ophthalmologist	oftalmol	oftalmólogo
orchi	orchiectomy	orqui	orquiectomía
oste	osteoarthritis	oste	osteoarthritis
ot	otolaryngology	ot	otorrinolaringología
ov	ovarian	ov	ovario
pancreat	pancreatic	pancreat	pancreático
path	homeopathic	pat	homeopático
ped	pediatrics	ped	pediatría
pel	pelvis	pel	pélvico
peps	pepsin	peps	pepsina
phag	esophagus	fag	esófago
phalang	phalange	falang	falange
pharyng	pharyngitis	faring	faringitis
phleb	phlebotomy	fleb	flebotomía
phob	phobia	fob	fobia
pneu	pneumonia	pne	neumonía
pod	podiatry	pod	podología
poster	posterior	poster	posterior
proct	proctologist	proct	proctólogo
psych	psychology	psic	psicología
pub	puberty	pub	pubertad
pyel	pyelography	piel	pielografía
radi	radiology	radi	radiología
rect	rectal	rect	rectal
ren	renal	ren	renal
retin	retina	retin	retina
rhin	rhinitis	rin	rinitis
salping	salpingectomy	salping	salpingectomía
sarc	sarcoma	sarc	sarcoma
sclero	sclerosis	escler	esclerosis
spermat	spermatozoon	espermat	espermatozoide

ENGLISH ROOT	ENGLISH EXAMPLE	SPANISH ROOT	SPANISH EXAMPLE
spin	spine	espin	espina
splen	splenectomy	spleen	esplenectomía
therap	therapist	terap	terapista
therm	thermometer	term	termómetro
thorac	thoracic	torac	torácica
thromb	thrombosis	tromb	trombosis
trache	trachea	traque	tráquea
troph	atrophy	trof	atrofia
tympan	tympanic	timpan	timpánica
umbilic	umbilical	umbilic	umbilical
ur	urinary	ur	urinario
urethr	urethra	uretr	uretra
vas	vascular	vas	vascular
ventr	ventricule	ventr	ventrículo
vertebr	vertebral	vertebr	vertebral
viscer	visceral	viscer	visceral

7 MEDICAL PREFIXES

ENGLISH	SPANISH
a	a
an	an
ante	anter
dia	dia
endo	endo
epi	epi
ex	ex
exo	exo
hiper	hyper
hipo	hypo
in	en
infra	infra
inter	inter
logy	logia
macro	macro
micro	micro
mono	mono
neo	neo
para	para
peri	peri
poly	poly
post	post
pro	pro
re	re
retro	retro
semi	semi
sub	sub
supra	supra
syn	sin
tachy	taqui
trans	trans

8 MEDICAL SUFFIXES

ENGLISH	SPANISH
ac	ac
al	al
algia	algia
cyte	cito
eal	eo
ectomy	ectomia
emia	emia
genic	genico(a)
gram	grama
graphy	grafia
iac	iaco(a)
iacal	iaco(a)
ic	ico(a)
ist	ista
itis	itis
lepsy	lepsia
logy	logia
malacia	malacia
manual	manual
oid	oid
ologist	ologist
ology	ology
oma	opma
oma	oma
osis	osis
ostomy	ostomía
pathy	patía
pexy	pexia
plasm	plasmo
plast	plast
plegia	plegia
ptosis	ptosis
rhaphy	rrafía
rhea	rrea
rrhage	rragia
scope	scopio
stasis	stasis
tomy	tomía
type	tipo
y	ia

9 INTERPRETER PROTOCOL

1. **Introduce** yourself as the interpreter and inform the speakers (patient, family, healthcare providers) that you will interpret everything that is said.

2. **Position** yourself to facilitate communication and eye contact between the speakers. Depending on the layout, sit next to the patient, or at a point between the patient and provider.

3. **Speak** in the first person for all parties (e.g. "I have pain here" and "I will write a prescription.")

4. **Convey** the speaker's full message in the same tone and register.

5. **Utilize** tools such as note taking or dictionaries when helpful.

6. **Avoid** side conversations. If clarification is necessary, state that the interpreter is seeking clarification from, or providing clarification to, the other speaker.

7. **Exit** the room when the provider exits. If the patient has questions, defer to when a provider is present.

8. **Inform** the interpreter dispatcher or manager of any significant procedural complications.

9. **Observe** a recognized code of ethics[1] for medical interpreters.

Compiled from institutional experience and publicly available guides including the CDC's "Interpretation Guidelines"

[1] There are various recognized codes of ethics for medical interpreters, including "National Code of Ethics for Interpreters in Health Care" by the National Council on Interpreting in Health Care, the "International Medical Interpreters Association Code of Ethics", and "California Standards for Healthcare Interpreters."

”

ABOUT THE AUTHOR

Annalisa Nash Fernandez is a nationally certified medical interpreter, working in Spanish and Portuguese. She has a B.S. from Georgetown University, and is a candidate for a Master's degree in Language, Literature, and Translation from the University of Wisconsin, Milwaukee. Her articles have appeared in print publications including *Education Week*. Annalisa lives in Milwaukee, Wisconsin and can be reached at EthnicEthosBooks@gmail.com.

ACKNOWLEDGMENTS

This niche dictionary practically asked to be created. As a medical interpreter, I needed a more technical, yet compact, lexicographic tool than existed in the market. As a graduate student, I documented this literature gap in my research paper "Function-based Lexicographic Tools for Medical Interpreting in Spanish." As a candidate preparing for national medical interpreter certification exams, I subscribed to the technically detailed Spanish language videos from Nucleus Medical Media, and compiled a list of the more esoteric terms requiring memorization. The combination of the research paper and that terminology compilation is now this dictionary.

I am grateful to Dr. Francisco Oddone as the dictionary's editor and medical expert content reviewer. Having recently completed medical school at the Universidad Católica de Córdoba in Argentina, he has a keen eye and sharp mind for, and fresh academic perspective on, medical terminology. The additions and corrections made by Dr. Oddone were crucial in the production of this dictionary. His transformation of an interpreter's rendition into a medically accurate publication was invaluable. This was truly an international project: Dr. Oddone editing from Argentina, Muhammad Usman Nawaz compiling the data in Pakistan, and the creative minds at Pixel Studio designing the cover from Bosnia and Herzegovina.

– Annalisa Nash Fernandez

NOTES

1. Bravo, Marco A., Elfrieda H. Hiebert, and P. David Pearson. "Tapping the Linguistic Resources of Spanish–English Bilingual: The role of cognates in science." *Vocabulary acquisition: Implications for reading comprehension* (2007): 140-156. NY: Guilford.

2. Centers for Disease Control and Prevention (CDC). National Center for Health Statistics (NCHS). "Interpretation Guidelines." Hyattsville, MD: U.S. Department of Health and Human Services, Centers for Disease Control and Prevention, 2006.

3. Cristoffanini, Paula, Kim Kirsner, and Dan Milech. "Bilingual lexical representation: The status of Spanish-English cognates." *The Quarterly Journal of Experimental Psychology* 38.3 (1986): 367-393.

4. *Nucleus Medical Media Catalog of Animations.* Nucleus Medical Media Inc., 2015.

5. Pirkola, Ari, Jarmo Toivonen, Heikki Keskustalo, and Kalervo Järvelin. "Frequency-based Identification of Correct Translation Equivalents (FITE) Obtained through Transformation Rules." *ACM Transactions on Information Systems* 26.1 (2007).

6. Tarp, Sven. "What Should We Demand from an Online Dictionary for Specialized Translation?" *Lexicographica* 29.1 (2013): 146-62.

INTERPRETER NOTES

INTERPRETER NOTES

21276841R00061

Made in the USA
Middletown, DE
23 June 2015